G000129995

THE PAST II

Series Editors: C. C. Elc

THE TAMING OF DEMOCRACY

THE CONSERVATIVE PARTY, 1880–1924

THE PAST IN PERSPECTIVE

Series Editors: C. C. Eldridge and Ralph A. Griffiths

C. C. Eldridge is Reader in History at the University of Wales, Lampeter.

Ralph A. Griffiths is Professor of Medieval History at the University of Wales, Swansea.

Other titles in this series:

THE PAST IN PERSPECTIVE

THE TAMING OF DEMOCRACY

THE CONSERVATIVE PARTY,
1880–1924

Jeremy Smith

CARDIFF
UNIVERSITY OF WALES PRESS
1997

© Jeremy Smith, 1997

British Library Cataloguing-In-Publication Data.
A catalogue record for this book is available from the British
Library.

ISBN   (paperback) 0-7083-1402-3
       (cased) 0-7083-1434-1

Typeset at the University of Wales Press
Printed in Great Britain by Dinefwr Press, Llandybïe

Contents

Editors' Foreword

Each volume in this series, *The Past in Perspective*, deals with a major theme of British, European or World history. The aim of the series is to engage the interest of all for whom knowledge of the riches of the world's historical experience is a delight, and in particular to meet the needs of students of history in universities and colleges — and at comparatively modest cost.

Each theme is tackled at sufficient length and in sufficient depth to allow each writer both to advance our understanding of the subject in the light of the most recent research, and to place his or her approach in due perspective. Accordingly, each volume contains a historiographical chapter which assesses how interpretations of its theme have developed, and have been criticized, endorsed, modified or discarded. Each volume, too, includes a section of substantial excerpts from key original sources: this reflects the importance of allowing the reader to come to his or her own conclusions about differing interpretations, and also the greater accessibility nowadays of original sources in print. Furthermore, in each volume there is a detailed bibliography which not only underpins the writer's own account and analysis, but also enables the reader to pursue the theme, or particular aspects of it, to even greater depth; the explosion of historical writing in the twentieth century makes such guidance invaluable. By these perspectives, taken together, each volume is an up-to-date, authoritative and substantial exploration of themes, ancient, medieval or modern, of British, European, American or World significance, after more than a century of the study and teaching of history.

C. C. Eldridge and Ralph A. Griffiths

Explanatory note
Reference to the Illustrative Documents which follow the main text

are indicated by a bold roman numeral preceded by the word 'DOCUMENT', all within square brackets [**DOCUMENT XII**].

Acknowledgements

Many thanks to Malcolm Smith and Stuart Ball for reading earlier drafts, and to the History Department of University of Wales, Lampeter, for providing a friendly atmosphere in which to write. Above all, to Charlie, Tigey and Pud for keeping me sane.

Jeremy Smith
1996

1.   The Conservative Party and
the Historians

From our perspective at the end of the twentieth century, the dominant theme of modern British politics has been the continued success of the Conservative party. Between 1924 and 1996 it has occupied government, either alone or as the senior partner, for fifty-three of the seventy-two years. Of the eighteen general elections during this period the party has won eleven, gaining a working majority each time with an overall average of 45 per cent of the vote. By contrast the Labour party has won seven elections, gaining a House of Commons majority only twice, in 1945 and 1966, with an overall average of 39 per cent of the vote. The once-mighty Liberal party has not won any elections and has not formed a government, though Liberal ministers sat in the 1931, 1935 and 1940 national governments. By any standards the twentieth century could well be described as a 'Conservative Century' (A. Seldon and S. Ball, *Conservative Century: The Conservative Party since 1900*).

Such dominance was not always the case. If we step back forty years to 1885, a very different perspective emerges. 'I confess much doubt', Michael Hicks Beach, the Conservative chief secretary for Ireland, wrote to the prime minister, Lord Salisbury, 'whether the country can be governed nowadays by persons holding opinions which you and I should call even moderately conservative.' His pessimism was well founded. Since 1830 Liberal parties had dominated government, relinquishing their seals of office only, for the most part, when they quarrelled with each other, as in 1834, 1852, 1858, 1866 and 1885. At just two of the fourteen general elections between 1831 and 1885 did the Tories win, in 1841 and 1874, both majorities being comprehensively wiped out at the following contest. The Conservative party resembled a permanent opposition rump impeded by a seemingly immovable Liberal ascendancy, based on support from the 'commercial middle-classes, Whig landowners, small shop-keepers and skilled artisans', rooted firmly in the cultural and moral values of the age.

This spotlights the forty years between the party's pre-1885 minority status and its post-1924 dominance as a transitional period of critical significance. At the heart of this transition lay the party's shift from a narrowly aristocratic, landed and paternalistic group of parliamentarians, based on tightly controlled county constituencies, into its modern form as a predominantly middle-class, suburban, property-owning, low-tax and small-state party. This adaptation provoked intense strains and shifting political fortunes. Of the twelve elections between 1885 and 1924, the Tories won six, achieving an independent party majority on just three occasions – in 1895, 1922 and 1924. During this period they won their highest independent tally of seats this century, with 429 in 1924, but also suffered their worst ever defeat, in 1906, which initiated their longest period of continuous opposition, between 1905 and 1915. And although they occupied government for twenty-four of the forty years, all of this, apart from ten months in 1922–3, was in alliance with Ulster Unionists and a breakaway Liberal segment: firstly with the Liberal Unionists in 1886–92 and 1895–1905, then with the coalition Liberals under Lloyd George between 1916 and 1922. Clearly, the road to 1924 was an uncertain one. Indeed, at certain moments (1903–6, 1911–14, 1918 and 1922–3), it seemed the party might not survive at all, either being subsumed or perishing altogether as every other late nineteenth-century continental party of the right had done. How it avoided expiry and how Conservatives established themselves as the dominant force in British politics will be a central theme of this short work.

Despite this extraordinary electoral record, the party has been strangely ignored. If history is written by the winners, then historians of the Conservative party have been slow to collect their prize. Whilst an immense corpus of literature exists on the Labour and Liberal parties, relatively little serious research had been undertaken on the Conservative party before the late 1960s and to some extent not until the mid-1970s. This is not altogether surprising. Academic attention has always orientated towards the more energetic and 'activist' forces in society (hence the upsurge of interest in Conservative subjects since Mrs Thatcher). Also, Conservatism was popularly equated with simple resistance and the party was considered a refuge for reactionaries, the insecure, the selfish, the blinkered and the out-of-date, thus making 'the stupid party' a subject almost unworthy of serious academic study.

Because of this lack of academic interest before the 1960s, the few studies there were of the party tended to be narrow and inadequate. One source was retired Conservative politicians, whose overly impressionistic accounts were designed to carve for themselves a place in history or used as a platform for personal recrimination, such as Lord Beaverbrook's trilogy on Conservative politics during and after the Great War: *Politicians and the War, 1914–1916* (1928–32); *Men and Power 1917–1918* (1956); and *The Decline and Fall of Lloyd George* (1963). Others sought to legitimate a particular brand of Conservatism, as with Maurice Woods's *The History of the Tory Party* (1924); Henry Cavendish-Bentinck's, *Tory Democracy* (1918); A. Bryant's *The Spirit of Conservatism* (1929); and Walter Elliott's *Toryism and the Twentieth Century* (1927). Alternatively, Conservative politics were written either through self-exonerating memoirs or collections of letters, as with those of Walter Long, Austen Chamberlain, the earl of Midleton, A. Griffith-Boscawen and Willoughby de Broke, or they were written through eulogistic biographies by relatives. The latter category included: Blanche Dugdale's *Arthur James Balfour* (1936); Winston Churchill's *Lord Randolph Churchill* (1906); Lady Gwendolen Cecil's *The Life of Robert, Marquis of Salisbury* (1921–32); Viscount Chilston's *Chief Whip: 1st Lord Chilston* (1961); V. Hicks Beach's *The Life of Sir Michael Hicks Beach* (1932) and the 2nd earl of Birkenhead's *Frederick Edwin, Earl of Birkenhead* (1933).

During the 1950s and 1960s studies of the Conservative party and Conservative topics became, for the first time, areas of academic inquiry. The party's return to power in 1951, and domination of government for the next thirteen years under the liberal Conservatism of Churchill, Eden, Macmillan and Butler, encouraged research on similar centre-left Conservative themes. In particular, Disraeli, with his rhetorical sympathy for working-class conditions and Tory democracy, appeared to echo many of the aspirations of Conservatism in the 1950s and 1960s, objectives that seemed to require restatement after Labour's 1964 victory and the revival of libertarian, new right ideas within the party: hence Robert Blake's *Disraeli* (1966); P. Smith's *Disraelian Conservatism and Social Reform* (1967); M. Cowling's *1867, Disraeli, Gladstone and Revolution* (1967); E. Feuchtwanger's *Disraeli, Democracy and the Tory Party* (1968); and H. Hanham's *Elections and Party Management: Politics in the Time of Disraeli and Gladstone* (1969). Others looked at these questions from more sociological directions, focusing in particular on Disraeli's attempt to attach the working classes to the party: hence R. McKenzie and A. Silver's *Angels in Marble* (1967) and E. Nordlinger's *The Working-Class Tories* (1967).

The consensual political atmosphere also encouraged a more sympathetic treatment for that pre-eminently centrist Tory, Stanley Baldwin, with J. Raymond's *The Baldwin Age* (1960); K. Middlemas and J. Barnes's enormous biography, *Baldwin* (1969); K. Middlemas (ed.), *T. Jones: A Diary with Letters* (1969); and R. R. James, *Memoirs of a Conservative: J. C. C. Davidson's Life and Papers* (1969). The contemporary mood encouraged biographical attention for previous constructively-minded Conservatives, such as Randolph Churchill (by R. R. James) and Joe Chamberlain (by P. Fraser and the remaining three volumes of the official biography by Julian Amery). This concentration upon biography and memoirs was understandable. If the common assumption was that Conservative government amounted to little more than pragmatism, then the craft of governing, statecraft, was best studied by examining the lives of statesmen, in other words through biography. This emphasis upon the craft of governing also helps to explain why there were few thoroughgoing analyses of Conservative ideology and its relation to Conservative politics, the two seemingly floating free of each other.

The upsurge of interest during the 1960s was finally brought together by Robert Blake in a general survey for his Ford Lectures of 1968, published as *The Conservative Party from Peel to Churchill* (1970) and later extended to include the years from 1955 to 1983. Despite now being over twenty-five years old, the work remains an excellent starting-point, though with the passage of time its deficiencies have become more apparent, in particular its infusion with a Whiggish confidence. Blake was to be an important influence on writing about the Conservative party, encouraging many young historians, most notably John Ramsden, and co-editing a four-volume series (recently extended to six) on the history of the Conservative party, to which R. Stewart and J. Ramsden contributed two volumes by the late 1970s: respectively, *The Foundation of the Conservative Party, 1830–1867* (1978), and *The Age of Balfour and Baldwin, 1902–1940* (1978). In addition, with the return of the Conservatives to government from 1970 to 1974 others followed Blake in offering wider surveys of the party. Of particular interest are R. Southgate, *The Conservative Leadership, 1832–1932* (1974), T. Lindsay and M. Harrington, *The Conservative Party, 1918–1970* (1974), and A. Gamble, *The Conservative Nation* (1974).

The 1970s were also a period of acute party turmoil. Two election defeats in 1974 prompted the replacement of Heath with Thatcher in 1975. Her subsequent election as prime minister in 1979 shifted the party firmly to the right, thereby injecting a large measure of doctrinal heat into what had traditionally been a rather practical and utilitarian approach to policy matters. As a result, Conservative politics became polarized between the pragmatic, liberal, old guard and the new, ideological, right-wing *enragés*, in a manner not witnessed since the Edwardian splits over tariff reform. Such internal political conflict proved immensely stimulating for writing and research on Conservative topics. Some of this interest was engaged directly in fighting for the soul of the Conservative party. Thus, in defence of the old order Ian Gilmour published *Inside Right* (1977), a shrewd and erudite censure of new right Conservatism, as was, to a less obvious extent, Lord Butler (ed.), *The Conservatives* (1977). Others sought to legitimate the new, or some of the new, doctrinal Conservatism: these included M. Cowling (ed.), *Conservative Essays* (1978); the same author's *Religion and Public Doctrine in Modern England* (1980); and R. Scruton, *The Meaning of Conservatism* (1980).

The encouragement for studying Conservative topics provided by political developments during the 1970s and early 1980s was especially powerful in stimulating research into the party of the late nineteenth and early twentieth centuries. This originated in the perception of a shared political idiom between the party of Thatcher and the party of the late-Victorian and Edwardian period: a belief that both epochs grappled with similar social, economic and even constitutional questions. These included anxieties about Britain's economic position, her place in the world, a debate over the role of the state and welfare provision which fed through into a concern for the moral vitality of the British people, rising trade union militancy and how to respond to it, apprehension at constitutional developments and a paranoia at Britain's decline. Interest in the party of the late nineteenth and early twentieth centuries was also a consequence of a growing exhaustion, by the mid-1980s, in the debate over the rise of Labour and concomitant decline of the Liberal party. As this controversy increasingly ran into the sand, historical investigation began to focus instead upon the late-Victorian and Edwardian Conservative party.

This attention was much broader in its basis of study than the previous, rather narrow concentration upon the parliamentary party and its 'great' leaders. For example, the evolution of Conservative ideas was investigated in F. O'Gorman *British Conservatism from Burke to Thatcher* (1985); W. Greenleaf, *The British Political Tradition: The Ideological Inheritance* (1983); G. Webber, *The Ideology of the British Right, 1918–1939* (1986); and R. Eccleshall *English Conservatism since the Reformation* (1990). Other studies focused on Conservative policy, particularly economic policy with A. Sykes, *Tariff Reform in British Politics* (1979); A. Offer, *Property and Politics, 1870–1914* (1981); M. Fforde's idiosyncratic *Conservatism and Collectivism, 1886–1914* (1990); and E. Green's *The Crisis of Conservatism* (1995); or defence and imperial policy with R. Williams, *Defending the Empire: The Conservative Party and British Defence Policy* (1991); and A. Friedberg, *The Weary Titan* (1988). Some of the most interesting work has looked at the influence of pressure groups, constituency parties or various back-bench movements. These include S. Ball, *Baldwin and the Conservative Party* (1988); F. Coetzee, *For Party or Country* (1990); M. Pugh, *The Tories and The People* (1985); G. Phillips, *The Diehards* (1979); and J. Ridley, 'The Unionist Social Reform Committee: Wets before the deluge', *Historical Journal*, 1987.

Several fruitful developments resulted from this historical attention. One has been the 'rediscovery' of Lord Salisbury, previously a much underrated and ignored leader, yet one who held the prime ministership for longer than anyone since 1827 and whose record would suggest that he was, arguably, the most successful Conservative leader ever. This interest has taken many forms, from *The Salisbury Review*, a hagiographical right-wing journal, to studies more worthy of serious attention such as P. Marsh, *The Discipline of Popular Government* (1978); Lord Blake and H. Cecil, *Salisbury: The Man and his Policies* (1987); and, more recently, E. Green's *The Crisis of Conservatism, 1880–1914* (1995); and R. Shannon's *The Age of Salisbury, 1881–1902* (1996). Appropriately enough, Andrew Roberts is currently working on the first official biography of Salisbury.

Another consequence has been a growing debate over the condition of the Edwardian Conservative party. Taking up where the decline of the Liberal party controversy ran out of steam, many historians have argued that it was the Tory party which faced an acute crisis in the years preceding the Great War. According to this view, the party was increasingly weakened by the encroachment of democracy, the problem of national finance and taxation caused by imperial, economic and social tensions and the effectiveness of the

Liberal–Labour electoral pact which the Conservatives found impossible to dislodge. Indeed, the conclusion of many studies – particularly A. Sykes, *Tariff Reform in British Politics*; M. Pugh, *The Making of Modern British Politics, 1867–1939* (1982); E. Green, 'Radical Conservatism: The electoral genesis of Tariff Reform', *Historical Journal*, 1985; M. Fforde, *Conservatism and Collectivism, 1886–1914* (1990); D. Dutton, *His Majesty's Loyal Opposition, 1905–1915* (1992) and E. Green, *The Crisis of Conservatism, 1880–1914* – is that the very survival of the party was in serious doubt on the eve of war. On the other hand a more positive view is taken by J. Ramsden, *The Age of Balfour*; with G. Searle, 'The revolt from the right' in P. Kennedy and A. Nichols (eds.), *Nationalist and Racialist Movements* (1981); and F. Coetzee, *For Party and Country*, who all in varying degrees question the degree of party crisis by 1914.

One of the more interesting features of the 'crisis of Conservatism' debate has been investigation of a radical right-wing group within the Conservative party, which displayed clear affinities with continental right-wing movements and espoused mildly proto-fascist ideas. Interest in this area grew out of contemporary developments under Thatcher, as well as a growing concern amongst historians of Germany about the nature of the German pre-war radical right and its connection to the origins of Nazism – the so-called 'Sonderweg debate'. Under these stimulants studies of the British radical right have included G. Searle, 'Critics of Edwardian society: the case of the radical right', in A. O'Day (ed.), *The Edwardian Age* (1979); G. Phillips, 'Lord Willoughby de Broke and the politics of radical Toryism', *Journal of British Studies* (1980); A. Sykes, 'The radical right and the crisis of Conservatism before the First World War', *Historical Journal* (1983); G. Phillips, *The Diehards*; F. Coetzee, *For Party and Country*; and E. Green's *The Crisis of Conservatism, 1880–1914*. An important effect of this specific line of enquiry has been to undermine the rather smug satisfaction of Conservative party enthusiasts and, more generally, those wedded to a Whiggish understanding of the evolution of the British state and political system. The new analysis suggests that developments this side of the channel were not automatically so successful, progressive or tolerant as was previously thought, nor was the shape of change so different from events on the Continent.

The outpouring of research on the Conservative party in the 1980s and 1990s has recently been brought together in a comprehensive thematic collection, edited by A. Seldon and S. Ball,

Conservative Century: The Conservative Party Since 1900 (1994), with
two other general histories of the party since the late nineteenth
century, one by John Charmley and the other, *The Conservatives in
British Society, 1880–1980*, edited by M. Francis and I. Zweiniger-
Bargielowska published shortly after this text went to press. Yet
despite the growth in research, several important areas remain very
lightly ploughed. Local studies are a large void in Conservative
history, especially when compared with the solid mass that exists for
both the Labour and Liberal parties. A few steps have been made in
this direction by J. Lawrence, T. Jeffrey and in a recent doctorate by
F. Aubel on Welsh Conservatism, but clearly at a local level 'the
Conservative half of society is still largely awaiting its historians' (M.
Pugh, *The Tories and the People*, 5). Secondly, the employment of new
historical perspectives to Conservative subjects has been relatively
slow, especially the application of gender theory. Some work in this
area is now being undertaken, notably by J. Lawrence and D. Jarvis,
but much remains to be done in this important field. Lastly, a
significant point was raised by B. Coleman in his *Conservatism and
the Conservative Party in the Nineteenth Century* (1988): various
'Conservatizing' agencies within society, such as the Church, the law,
governmental institutions, the civil service and the military, all need
greater historical scrutiny if we are to understand the party's survival
and success.

2. Conservative Party Organization and Ideology

Party organization

The Conservative party has been compared to a command structure, hierarchically assembled, with power concentrated at the top in the leader who 'ruled from on high', with directives flowing downwards to the different levels of operation, all working towards the common goal of electoral success (R. Eccleshall et al., *Political Ideologies*, 74). This analogy has much to recommend it. If we take the question of leadership, then according to McKenzie 'the most striking feature . . . is the enormous power which appears to be concentrated in the hands of the leader' (R. McKenzie, *British Political Parties*, 21). This power included the right to formulate party policy, to dispense patronage, to recommend Cabinet appointments to the Crown, to select junior ministers and to invite colleagues onto the front bench. He also enjoyed security of tenure.

On closer scrutiny, such a representation of the leadership appears overly simple. For example, although no formal mechanism of reselection (removal) emerged until 1965, in practice tenure was vulnerable to informal procedures. Back-bench sniping and dissension, especially if covertly supported by elements within the leadership, could undermine a party leader, as happened to both Northcote (1881–4) and Balfour (1909–11). Austen Chamberlain in 1922 also faced a rebellious alliance of back-benchers and junior ministers. Sometimes dissension could harden into a more permanent movement or group. Balfour's retirement was hastened by opposition from the mutinous Halsbury group and the 'Balfour must Go' crusade of Leo Maxse. Chamberlain was similarly undermined at the hands of the Anti-Waste campaign of 1920–2, while Bonar Law, though surviving, was almost toppled by the Unionist Business Committee in 1916. The period following an election defeat was always a difficult moment for the party leader, though not necessarily a fatal one. Disraeli survived moves to oust him following the 1868 defeat. Salisbury faced little problem after 1892, Baldwin weathered the 1923 setback, and it took three election defeats finally to unseat Balfour.

A similar misconception occurs with regard to a leader's power to determine party policy. Certainly he would set the party tone, as Disraeli did in 1872 at the Crystal Palace, Bonar Law in 1912 at Blenheim Palace, or Baldwin in 1925 with his 'Give us peace in our time' speech. But policy, as with the distribution of patronage, was a product not of autonomous contemplation but of balancing numerous party interests. It required close communication with colleagues of high standing and regard for prevailing sentiments and groupings in the parliamentary party, as well as regard for political circumstances and, to a lesser extent, opinion in the wider party organization. After all, the Conservative leader 'retains power only with the consent of his followers' (McKenzie, *British Political Parties*, 22): to ignore these interests could invite disagreement and corrode status.

Tory leaders worked through inner cabinets or ruling cliques of influential party elders and operators. Disraeli leaned heavily for guidance on the fifteenth earl of Derby, Cairns and his personal secretary, Montagu Corry. Salisbury and Balfour drew counsel from within the charmed circle of their Hotel Cecil. Bonar Law sought the advice of Balfour, Long, Lord Balcarres (the chief whip) and Beaverbrook before any move. Similarly Baldwin was close to J. C. C. Davidson and Walter Bridgeman. Leaders also began to call meetings of ex-ministers to discuss party matters, which became formalized after 1906 when Balfour summoned 'shadow' cabinets on a regular basis. These could act at times as a brake on a leader's independent action and authority, as in July 1911 when Balfour's Shadow Cabinet split over tactics towards the Parliament Bill, with the malcontents subsequently joining the rebels. In any case, whether formally or informally constituted, there existed an almost natural inclination for Tory leaders to confer widely and proceed by consensus: they have usually, but not exclusively, emerged from the centre of the party and reached the top post because of their unifying qualities and appeal to a broad range of Conservative opinion.

For much of this period the position of party leader had no statutory or legislative definition to its role and powers. Before 1922, the party leadership was shared between leaders in the Commons and the Lords. If either was an ex-prime minister then he became the overall party leader, as Salisbury did after 1892 and Balfour after 1906. But if no ex-prime minister existed, as with Northcote and Salisbury from 1881 to 1885 and Bonar Law, firstly with Lansdowne (1911–16), then with Curzon (1916–21), the division of responsibility and power was ambiguous. Leaders were therefore informally checked in the exercise of their power by various countervailing pressures. Instead of a 'Hobbesian model of party leadership', we are encouraged, in one prominent analysis of the topic, to perceive it as more akin to that of the 'head of the household' (P. Norton and A. Aughey, *Conservatives and Conservatism*, 241–2).

Sustaining the leader was the parliamentary party. A distinctly Conservative party had existed at Westminster since 1828, when Wellington was called to form his ministry, so forcing out the more liberal Canningites. In the aftermath of the Reform crisis and the collapse in Tory support at the 1832 election, Sir Robert Peel, the new leader in the Commons, sought to reunify and reinvent the party. He offered a refashioned Burkean vision with his Tamworth Manifesto, in place of the party's reactionary image, and projected himself as a responsible, sound minister working with, and not against, contemporary social and economic trends (as he tried to show during his brief 1834 ministry). Peel might have succeeded in this strategy had he not been brought down by a back-bench revolt from the more Tory sections of the party, who claimed Peel was undermining both the Anglican Church and the Aristocratic Constitution by the Maynooth Grant and repeal of the Corn Laws. The revolt split the party. The entire front bench of about eighty aligned with the Whigs and Radicals in what became the Liberal party by the late 1850s. The remainder of the party, though more explicitly Tory for the first time since 1830, was consigned to almost permanent opposition interspersed with a few brief spells of minority government. After 1846 many in the Conservative party looked for reunion with the Peelites, but this proved impossible while Disraeli remained leader in the Commons. The position was made worse by the death of Palmerston in 1865 and the political polarization that resulted from Gladstone's first ministry in 1868. From 1868, we can observe a fairly stable Conservative parliamentary existence, though one still locked in a position of minority status.

Stability did not, however, mean homogeneity. The party was a heterogeneous mix, comprising the front-bench leadership, those holding minor government posts, such as junior ministers or PPSs, ex-ministers, unambitious county squires and retired military officers or bankers capping their career with the social kudos of being an MP, and the rising career politicians and aspiring young men eager for preferment. These distinct 'types' would look to a front-bencher of their hue as their champion: the middle-class businessmen to George Goschen or W. H. Smith, the 'squires' to Henry Chaplin and Walter Long, the 'young men' to George Wyndham and, after 1906, to F. E. Smith. In compositional terms the party was more homogeneous. In 1885, it was predominantly of a landed and aristocratic background; by 1906 larger numbers of business/professional men were entering the party, with Bonar Law being the first 'man of trade' to assume the leadership.

To connect the leadership to the parliamentary party was the role of the chief whip and the whips' office, of about five or six influential members, described as 'the essential communicative buckle that linked backbenchers . . . with an increasingly organised front bench' (A. Seldon and S. Ball, *Conservative Century*, 101). Their role was one of communication, management and discipline: communication of opinions and feeling between front and back benches, warning leaders of party unease and informing back-benchers of the leadership's intentions. They also communicated with coalition partners, with the Liberal Unionists or Lloyd George Liberals. In addition, they managed business in the House, arranged pairing, gave notice for divisions or important debates, organized speakers and talent-spotted. Furthermore, until 1911 whips took charge of electoral management outside the House, distributing funds to constituencies and assisting in the search for candidates. Ultimately, the whips were there to discipline. They sought to preserve loyalty to the leadership and support in the division lobbies through a formal process of line-whips and, more informally, through reasoned argument, the offer of preferment, threats of demotion or being sidelined for office, the removal of financial support and the creation of difficulties within constituencies.

However, back-benchers were not completely craven-hearted or powerless in the face of the coercive power of the whips. Something of the independent member spirit survived amongst more traditional sections on the back benches. And if a member had the backing of his local party then he was generally secure, the selection and de-selection of candidates being the prime responsibility of local constituencies. There were also techniques for signifying discontent to the leadership. Unofficial bodies were an effective way of registering protest and challenging the ruling élite. The Fourth Party, led by Randolph Churchill, ended Northcote's hopes of the prime ministership and forced the leadership into a more partisan stance. The Halsbury Club of 1911 also sought to ginger up the leadership and may have helped to remove Balfour later in the year. Deputations, back-bench memorials or letters to *The Times* were also used to indicate misgivings, as were start-of-session dinners and party meetings which, as in the case of 1922, could turn into spectacular rebuffs of the official leadership. More public, and only employed if private methods met with little satisfaction, was abstention or voting against the leadership in a major division. The Nigeria debate of November 1916 forced the Tory leader, Bonar Law, to move against Asquith and, eventually, into coalition with Lloyd George, after his back-bench support collapsed from 186 to just seventy-three.

Underpinning the party at Westminster was the party organization in the country. Following the 1832 Reform Act various constitutional associations, Conservative Working Men's Clubs and registration societies emerged in boroughs to organize and administer support and to oversee the enlarged electoral register. Though voluntary and jealous of their independence from central party control, these associations did receive some party funds at election times, distributed by a Carlton Club committee of party elders and the chief whip. The 1867 expansion of the franchise in the boroughs increased the number of associations and clubs as pressure was generated to manage these new and largely alien electorates. But party organization appeared chaotic, with borough associations and clubs operating independently of one another and separated by class distinctions, whilst county constituencies remained outside the party structure altogether and under the firm influence of local interests. The combination of these difficulties with the prospect of an election in the near future prompted an attempt to co-ordinate activity at a local and national level: hence the creation in 1867 of the National Union of Conservative and Constitutional Associations by Henry Raikes.

Initially shunned by many constituency associations sensitive of their autonomy, and by a Tory leadership dismissive of its explicitly middle-class, borough membership and fearful of its popular undertones, the National Union's value in providing the party with a mass organization soon made itself felt. More associations affiliated (289 by 1871 and 472 by 1875) as its importance increased. The

National Union flourished at a local branch level, as an electoral vehicle for the party, mobilizing support, canvassing opinion and distributing propaganda, engaging the enthusiastic foot-soldiers and activists of middle-class, borough Conservatism. It also helped to establish new constituency associations and Working Men's Clubs, paid for travelling lecturers, raised funds, and opened a direct channel of communication from the leadership to the wider party to disseminate guidance, advice and policy. But, unlike both the Liberal and Labour parties, the National Union did not intend to rival the parliamentary party's authority or even discuss policy matters; rather, in the words of Henry Raikes, it was simply the 'hand-maid to the party'.

Yet the hand-maid could sometimes behave like the housewife. The channel of communication that the Union provided enabled the disenchantment of the grass roots to filter upwards to the leadership. In the early 1880s this manifested itself as pent-up middle-class Conservative frustration at lethargic aristocratic leadership and domination of the party's upper reaches. It also took the remarkable turn of Randolph Churchill, vice-president of the Union, calling in 1883 for the democratization of party organization. Churchill sought to endow the National Union with the powers of a caucus, over policy, finance and candidatures, thus 'taking it out of the hands of a self-elected body'. Although unsuccessful, it was an early example of that stock-broker, blue-rinse, grass-roots Conservative reaction that would be common throughout the twentieth century. It also allowed the nobly-born Churchill to rise to prominence in the party and win himself a place at Salisbury's highly aristocratic Cabinet table in 1885.

In addition, National Union influence was located in the party conference, which provided a ready platform for the advocacy of policy initiatives, often in opposition to those of the leadership. In the 1880s, for example, conference demanded help for working men to purchase their own homes and for Fair Trade, much to the annoyance of Salisbury. Balfour, in the face of a tabled amendment for the Leeds conference on 16 November 1911 criticizing his leadership, resigned on 9 November. And at party conferences between 1920 and 1922 opposition to the coalition and demands for a reassertion of independent Conservative government were regularly expressed.

It was fear of this increasingly assertive and grass roots element in the Conservative party that prompted the centre to strengthen the hold of the parliamentary leadership over the party. In 1870, Disraeli appointed John Gorst as principal agent of a new Conservative Central Office, under the authority of the ruling Central Committee of aristocratic party elders, with the intention of equipping the party with a professional organization. This included 'checking registration lists, assisting in finding suitable candidates, circulating literature, encouraging the formation of local associations, maintaining election statistics, liaising with the press and advising . . . electoral procedure' (P. Norton and A. Aughey, *Conservatives and Conservatism*, 223). This remit overlapped somewhat with the National Union, as was perhaps the intention, leaving areas of potential conflict and tension. Any immediate demarcation dispute was avoided by the appointment of Gorst as secretary of the National Union in 1871 and by placing the Union and Central Office under the same roof in Smith Square in 1872. These moves co-ordinated activity and played an important role in the 1874 election victory, though the organization quickly fell into disrepair. Not until Captain Middleton took over as principal agent in 1886 did Central Office once again fulfil its early promise. In 1911, after three election defeats and a massive increase in the workload, several key reforms were pushed through. The most significant was the creation of a chairman of the party, the first being A. Steel-Maitland, in charge of Central Office, whilst the chief whip, Lord Balcarres from 1911 to 1913, was to occupy himself solely with parliamentary business. A new post of party treasurer was also created to oversee fund-raising and expenses.

However, centralization nourished strains between the core and the periphery and between the official and the voluntary sides of the party. Central Office was keen to extend control over the party machine, especially when confronted by the increasingly assertive National Union and with central funds filtering down to the local associations. The local constituencies, however, clung to their power-base, particularly the selection of candidates. With little central control, this left local constituencies vulnerable to entryism from various political groups, leagues and societies looking to alter the complexion of the party at Westminster. For example, the Tariff Reform League, through its shadowy and more radical arm, the Confederates, carried on a successful if bitter campaign at a local level to purge the constituencies of Unionist Free Traders. The Anti-Waste campaign of the early 1920s undertook similar tactics, though often the threat was sufficient to influence the party at Westminster.

On the other hand, the various leagues and single-issue societies, so important in rallying support to the party, often enjoyed close contact with Central Office and Conservative MPs. They struggled to educate the new democracy and equip it with direction and organization, though few of these bodies achieved a truly mass membership. The important exception was the Primrose League founded in 1883, the most successful and significant of these associations. By 1910, it constituted some 2,645 habitations with a total membership of over two million. Others included the Liberty and Property Defence League of the 1880s and the Anti-Socialist Union of 1907, both of which sought to rally voters against the evils of collectivism. The Fair Trade League, the Tariff Reform League and the Empire Free Trade crusade of the 1920s mobilized support for an internalized imperial market, sheltered from the bracing winds of a competitive world economy, whilst the Navy League, the National Maritime League and the National Service League struggled to rouse public apprehension over national security. These were all movements dedicated to organizing a larger, more independent and predominantly urban electorate behind issues associated with the Tory party. But they also performed a more vital function. All parties, if they are to win elections, must extend their appeal beyond the limited range of their own activists and enthusiasts, into the grey areas (sometimes called the centre-ground) of floating voters, the undecided, the marginals and the new voter. The collection of leagues and societies offered vital mechanisms for infusing and disseminating conservative-friendly values and prejudices into just these reaches of the electorate. They were Conservatizing agents operating beyond the reach of the Conservative party.

The Conservative party then, whilst showing some similarities with a military command structure, was also subject to conflict and tension between and within its different levels. Friction existed at most points: back bench versus front bench, local constituencies versus Central Office, National Union versus the leadership. What helped bind the various components together was a shared 'belief and value system', a shared body of ideas.

Ideas and ideology

Before the mid-1970s Conservatism was badly served by historians and philosophers. Many denied it was an ideology at all, 'not an ism' as one leading thinker has observed (I. Gilmour, *Inside Right*, 121).

Rather, it operated as 'a habit of mind, a mode of feeling, a way of living' and functioned, in political and policy terms, through empirical method, experience and common sense observation rather than the application of ideas to the demands of government (R. J. White, *The Conservative Tradition,* 1). A number of 'philosophical reference points' or 'abiding concerns' – or simply values – were pinpointed, but these held only a loose mooring to action and were subordinate to circumstance in shaping political behaviour (A. Aughey et al., *The Conservative Political Tradition in Britain and the United States,* 21). These 'abiding concerns' included a number of interlocking beliefs, at the core of which lay an aversion to change and a predisposition to conserve the existing order. This impulse was especially strong with those who felt that they had something to lose, whether it be land, property, the return on stocks and shares, a job, social position, or perhaps continued patronage and charity, or even just a perception of comfort and security, however divorced such perceptions were from the reality of their lives. **[DOCUMENT I]** This outlook was reinforced by a sceptical conception of human nature: human nature was flawed not only by its inability adequately to reason the world, and thus unable to improve it without injury to someone, but also by its capacity for evil and natural disposition to base passions, such as avarice, greed and envy. It was a view of human nature based on what A. Quinton has described as intellectual and moral 'imperfection'. This inclined such groups to value authority and order for the preservation of the present system, in which they felt comfortable and rewarded, thereby maintaining stability and regulating mankind's moral imperfection. Authority and order were located in the established governmental institutions, the Church, the existing legal system, the military, the father or husband.

Stability was also preserved, somewhat paradoxically, by accepting and guiding change; as Burke warned, 'a state without the means of some change is without the means of its conservation' (F. O'Gorman, *British Conservatism . . .,* 72). It was a question of gradually adjusting these established centres of authority to the shifting tempo of society – what Hugh Cecil has described as 'preservative change' (H. Cecil, *Conservatism,* 65). Maintaining the status quo was never a practical or even a desirable option for Conservatives. **[DOCUMENT II]** But it was self-restraint that upheld stability most effectively: hence Conservative attachment to traditional obligations and 'imagined' reverences – the Church, landlords, the monarchy, the locality or region, the nation, the family – all operating a form of psychological or cultural deterrence. We might add here property ownership, which also encouraged what Roger Scruton refers to as 'stable aspects': a sense of caution, independence, respect for others, especially their property, and an aversion to disorder and lawlessness (R. Scruton, *The Meaning of Conservatism*, 100). Conservatives have long sought the distribution of ownership within society as a method of anchoring the rootless, instilling responsibility and augmenting social forces opposed to rapid change, thus producing a powerful incentive for middle-class voters to rally behind the party.

The extension of property-ownership, along with attachments to traditional obligations, not only alleviated mankind's individual capacity for evil but limited its collective capacity as well. If mankind was defective in reason as well as prone to base passions, then government, as a practical operation of human reason, held great potential for mischief and damage to society whether in the form of despotism or majoritarian tyranny. To offset this menace, widespread property ownership and the multitude of personal loyalties, the 'little platoons', would provide a counterbalancing power. In addition, governments needed to be 'guided . . . by the accumulated political wisdom of the community', what Burke called 'the general bank and capital of nations and ages'. **[DOCUMENT III]** That bank came from a respect for the history and tradition of a particular society, with all its 'customary and established laws and institutions' and a strong constitution that limited the exercise of unrestricted power by either the Crown, the Commons, the Cabinet or the Lords. Government, according to Conservatives, was in the slightly incongruous position of having to be both a source of strength and resolution whilst limited and restrained in what it might actually accomplish.

Conservatives believed human nature to be not only naturally evil but also inherently unequal, every person being equipped with different abilities, skills and aspirations as reflected in the existing distribution of rewards and power. **[DOCUMENT IV]** This assumption led to several important conclusions. First, it ordained existing society with a natural sanction. Legitimacy rested with society as it was, not with how it might once have been in an original state of nature, invariably, according to radicals and dreamers who strove to recapture it, a state of nature where all were equal and all enjoyed natural rights. For Conservatives, established society (as with established authority) was legitimate simply because it was established. Individual rights could not, therefore, be natural or automatic because they had no authenticity beyond abstract theorizing. Rights could only be awarded and prescriptive, subordinate to existing duties and obligations especially to one's nation, family, Crown and state, rather than free-standing and inviolable as the Liberals asserted. Secondly, Conservative belief in (and appreciation of) inequality indicated that society was naturally hierarchical. Strong leadership from a competent ruling élite was therefore necessary and inevitable, beyond which everyone was entitled to discover their own particular station according to their own talents and desires. However, this essentially Liberal view contradicted Conservative convictions that society was more than just the sum of individuals and functioned as a whole, as an organism and 'a system of real relationships between individuals, classes, groups and interests' (R. J. White, *The Conservative Tradition*, 8). This led to the belief that under certain conditions government was allowed to ignore individual obligations and constitutional checks upon its power. The cause of national defence, for example, could justify overriding the rights and independence of property. Clearly, then, there is a tension running through Conservatism, identified by W. Greenleaf as being between a collectivist and a libertarian impulse.

Two things emerge from this brief survey. Firstly, Conservatism was (and is) more than simply a pragmatic and disinterested response to events: it is derived from and corresponds to 'a philosophical view of the nature of man, of society, and of the world' (P. Norton and A. Aughey, *Conservatives and Conservatism*, 18). In other words, Conservatives *were* moved by ideas and did operate with an idealized society lodged behind their pretensions to be un-ideological and 'grounded in practice'. The stimulus for redefining Conservatism as a doctrinal creed emerged in the mid-1970s, against a backdrop of a Conservative party and a Conservative government in which ideological baggage clearly drove political activity and exerted a powerful influence on policy initiatives. Secondly, Conservatism was not (and never has been) a fixed body of ideas, possessing 'a single, homogeneous character'. Rather, it ought to be likened to a repository of assorted values and traditions, shifting in terms of meaning and relevance, with points of overlap and areas of tension. Indeed, Conservative values were sufficiently diverse and plastic to unify the separate levels of the party organization and to attach people from different backgrounds, regions, ethnicity, classes, generations and gender to the party. As a composite form, it proved to be invaluable in allying the party with large sections of the electorate.

For the Conservative leadership, however, such an amorphous set of beliefs created problems. How, for example, should the leaders choose from this nebulous cluster of ideas when constructing a clear Conservative platform? What, from the assortment of values, should be prioritized or jettisoned in order to maximize the party's electoral appeal? In what form or manner should those values be presented and translated into practical statements? And how should the practical acts of governing be influenced by those beliefs? The problem, outlined by a prominent philosopher of Conservatism, is one of distinguishing between Conservative 'dogma' and Conservative 'policy', the former representing the depository of Conservative principles, the latter the distilled fruits of the politician. In this latter sense, Conservatism is a functional ideology, selected and deciphered from the wider bank of Conservative impulses and traditions, in order to win recruits, chime with broad popular sentiments and culture, inspire loyalty, guide political action and attract electoral support. Because it was functional, it was therefore manufactured and contextual, a representation and image fashioned according to a host of political variables, such as public opinion, economic conditions, contemporary political issues and developments, party composition, social changes, foreign affairs, the press, and numerous pressure groups and vested interests. To understand the ideology, we must therefore appreciate the context in which it is constructed.

The context between 1885 and 1924 was moulded by a number of developments. The collapse of agricultural prices hit the economic (and therefore political) power of landed wealth and impoverished rural labourers, injecting bitterness into landlord–tenant relations and threatening the former's ability, politically, to manage the counties. This process augmented rural migration and movement into the towns, reinforcing the significance of borough constituencies within the political system. This trend was rendered more alarming by a growing public awareness of large pockets of acute poverty and social distress in many British cities, and an increased willingness to implement collectivist policies to remedy them. The political environment was also shaped by the maturation of capitalism from the 1880s, strengthening the position of those traditionally Liberal groups, the financial and commercial interests, within the British Establishment. It also saw Britain's economic supremacy increasingly threatened by international competition. This encouraged commercial and industrial interest in imperial territories as a refuge for easy and stable markets, an interest that echoed growing popular support for empire. In addition, the Church of England faced renewed challenges from the growth of Non-conformity and Roman Catholicism, the removal of institutional benefits such as the tithe, and the general spread of secular values in British society. Perhaps most alarming for Conservatives was the steady advance of democracy, with extensions to the franchise in 1867, 1884, 1918 and 1928, the introduction of the secret ballot in 1872 and of the Corrupt and Illegal Practices Act in 1883. These changes opened up the 'stuffy' Victorian political system, undermining the more customary practices of political management and extending party organizations to supervise the larger and more 'independent' electorate. On top of these developments came alarming signs of self-reliance, if not defiance, in the populace: an assertive and agitational nationalist movement in Ireland, the appearance of various socialist clubs on mainland Britain, the growth of trade unionism, especially amongst non-craft, semi-skilled workers, and the rise of a Labour party with, by 1906, a solid presence at Westminster foreshadowing a new class-based politics.

Within this context, Tory leaders formulated a Conservative ideology that responded to the anxieties and tensions of a period of exceptional upheaval. Conservative ideology has always been at its sharpest and most dynamic when its core principles are under threat. The period from 1880 until 1924 was no exception. Conservatism therefore reacted to the challenges of the late nineteenth century by establishing a 'preservational' ideology, enabling the party to create a series of defensive alliances with numerous groups and individuals around a range of concerns. For instance, Conservatism increasingly displayed itself as the champion of freedom and individualism, given that both the Liberal and Labour parties were moving quickly in a collectivist direction, even though it too did not shrink from a dose of collectivism in the shape of tariff reform. Confronted by socialist agitation, industrial conflict, campaigns for disestablishment and Home Rule, and agrarian-inspired civil disobedience in Ireland, the Conservative party represented itself as the guardian of the social order and authority, upholding the union with Ireland (until 1921), the existing constitutional system, the Established Church, the integrity of the law and the rights of property and capital. From the 1880s onwards the party gathered the miscellaneous forms of capital and property under its wing, aligning the interests of middle-class, urban, industrial and commercial wealth with rural, landed and aristocratic interests in a common stand of defence and security. Defence and security of the empire were also appropriated by the party, drawing upon a sort of Pittite inheritance and sporadic expressions of popular sympathy on imperial issues. This stance generated much enthusiasm in the party, imbuing it with a sense of imperial mission and nationalistic pomp. Above all, the party characterized itself as standing for unification and what Frank O'Gorman refers to as 'consolidation' in an age of disintegration and discord: unity of the United Kingdom and social classes (although the party was increasingly becoming distinctly English and middle class), unity of 'the possessing classes' (those who owned property and capital), unity of the Anglican Church, and unity of the British Empire (F. O'Gorman, *British Conservatism* . . ., 40).

Of course things were never as unified or as clear-cut as this suggests. Given the assortment of Conservative values and traditions, it was unlikely, if not impossible, that just one 'Conservatism' could exist in the party. Instead, we can perceive several alternative representations of Conservative ideology operating at the same time. Usually these differed on points of emphasis or preference, but on occasions the fault-line could be an issue of substance and the difference unbridgeable and 'ideological'. This was clearly the case with the Unionist free-traders, who could find little common ground with 'whole-hogger' tariff reformers. Sometimes different representations would complement each other, but more often they would struggle for ascendancy in the party, at certain moments precipitating high-profile and public conflicts. Salisburian Conservatism, for example, was openly challenged by a more activist, middle-class variant from Randolph Churchill. From 1903, Balfourian Conservatism was confronted by a more dynamic and interventionist type advanced by Joseph Chamberlain and his tariff reform crusade. And during the last years of the coalition, the constructive approach of much of the leadership encountered problems from a more orthodox and traditional Conservatism. Frequently, alternative 'Conservatisms' were a consequence of conflicting regional priorities resulting from distinct socio-economic circumstances. Lancashire, with its cotton manufacturing and vigorous anti-Catholic and strongly working-class culture, clearly appreciated (and needed) a different brand of Conservative politics to that of an East Anglian market town, a leafy, middle-class suburb, or an East End borough. The heterogeneous mix of Conservatism allowed such dissimilar styles to reside together, but not always amicably.

Disunity in the party also resulted from the contrasting reactions of Tory politicians themselves. To some extent this was a question of tactics rather than of substance. Disagreement occurred over which values should be emphasized or when a particular course should be abandoned or advanced. Each political issue and encounter raised considerations of timing as well as of tactics, with individual Conservatives and the overall party balance falling one way or another according to direction from the leadership, personal ambition and perceptions of party and public opinion. However, some historians have generalized these tactical responses into categories of particular, and almost instinctive, Conservative 'species'. By one simple measure this would correlate to a left, centre, or right division (the latter advocating stout resistance and traditional appeals, perhaps corresponding to an older Tory mentality). Centrists, on the other hand, would back an approach of limited tinkering, whilst from the left would come support for pre-emptive strikes and 'dishing' the opposition. Other historians have cleaved the party into those of a 'doctrinal strain' and a 'positional element', what Glickman simplifies to 'die-hards and reactionaries' versus 'trimmers and realists' (H. Glickman, 'The Toryness of English Conservatism', *Journal of British Studies*, 1961). Following a similar distinction, Lord Butler distinguishes between 'dunderhead stand-patters' and the more 'supple and subtle intellectuals', no doubt including himself (Butler, *The Conservatives*, 9). A more sophisticated classification has pinpointed four categories: pessimistic Tories, paternalistic Tories, progressive Tories and combative Tories (P. Norton and A. Aughey, *Conservatives and Conservatism*, 53–90).

While Conservative politicians and leaders would locate themselves in a particular tradition, individuals could shift 'niches' or straddle several, if they were nimble or enigmatic enough (Randolph Churchill is a good example of such a protean Conservative). Nor was each tradition fixed in terms of what it represented or its party strength. It changed according to circumstances and the proclivities of the leader: under Lord Salisbury, pessimistic Toryism became the dominant party ethos, whilst in the years between 1906 and 1923 combative Toryism emerged as a powerful party posture. Baldwin later effected a return to an orthodox, consensual style of Conservatism. Therefore, Conservative ideology, as with Conservative organizations, contained within it innumerable points of conflict and tension. Sometimes these tensions fostered serious difficulties for the party. At other moments the leadership managed to suppress or marginalize such conflict. The party during the 1880s and 1890s displayed both these processes of conflict and management.

Salisbury and the Conservative Ascendancy, 1880–1900

Disunity and despair, 1880–1885

For many years historical opinion assumed that the Conservative party was rescued from its mid-Victorian wilderness by Disraeli. According to this view, Disraeli transformed the party from being narrowly aristocratic into a national party of all classes and regions. He also reinvented Conservatism: its sectional, protectionist, High-Church appeal was turned into a creed organized around defence of the monarchy, the Church, the empire and the nation, a creed that restored public trust in the party and returned it to government in 1874, its first majority since 1841. Recently, however, our picture of Disraeli has altered. In place of the Tory radical, Disraeli is now represented as a traditionalist upholding the aristocratic constitution and the dominance of the landed élite, whose reformist initiatives were largely rhetorical flourishes rather than acts of substance. His impact on the nineteenth-century Conservative party was far less significant than was once thought, as is apparent if we observe the party during the early 1880s, beset by an assortment of internal problems. Informed opinion was, at that time, more likely to consider the Tories to be in steady decline than revived and poised for office.

One source of difficulty was the question of leadership. The party's return to opposition following the 1880 election defeat, necessitating a firm lead to the despondent Tory MPs, was compounded by Disraeli's death in 1881 and his failure to promote an heir apparent. With no obvious replacement, the leadership was shared between Sir Stafford Northcote in the Commons and Lord Salisbury in the Lords. Neither proved entirely successful. Northcote was too prosaic and dispassionate to lead the party in opposition, especially against a radicalized Liberal government. He was a leader more suited to the rigours of administration and a ministerial brief than enthusing those behind him; and yet, in spite of these shortcomings, he remained the Queen's preferred choice as prime minister. This was less a reflection of Northcote's qualities than an awareness of Salisbury's defects. Salisbury had the pedigree and gravitas for leadership, but was thought to lack a sense of proportion and judgement; 'rash, headstrong, incautious, prejudiced' was how the *Pall Mall Gazette* described him in 1881. He was regarded, not unfairly after earlier assaults on Disraeli, as a reactionary, a vigorous defender of the aristocratic order, a fanatic on Church affairs and hostile to contemporary trends, and so not the ideal party leader for an increasingly democratic age.

The division of responsibility and clear ideological dissimilarity between Northcote and Salisbury quickly led to tactical problems, as over the Irish Land Act of 1881 and the Arrears Act of 1882, both of which left the opposition outmanœuvred by Gladstone and publicly humiliated. The temporary nature of the arrangement also encouraged others to advance their claims. In the Lords, Salisbury encountered trouble from Lord Cairns and the duke of Richmond. More seriously, Northcote was challenged in the Commons by Randolph Churchill and his small coterie of supporters, the Fourth Party, consisting of J. E. Gorst, Drummond-Woolf and Salisbury's nephew Arthur Balfour, a connection that clearly links Salisbury to Churchill's attempts to undermine Northcote. Churchill was a restless and flexible politician who used his debating ability and wit to assail the humourless Gladstone, win notoriety and support amongst Conservatives and belittle the pedestrian Northcote. Most dismissed him as an adventurer. But behind the fireworks lay calculating ambition: if he could usurp Northcote in the Commons, with the able but atavistic Salisbury marooned in the Lords, he would become the obvious choice as prime minister once the Tories returned to office.

All three leaders shared the same tactical goal of co-operation or fusion with a section of the Liberal party. However, they differed over how this might be achieved. Northcote offered a moderate approach to entice Whig malcontents into a centrist union with responsible Conservatives, a sort of Palmerstonian coalition, along similar lines to the operation of mid-Victorian governments. Churchill, on the other hand, recommended a more dynamic style, and a social reformist approach that he condensed into the slogan 'Tory democracy', a vague and vacuous combination of presumed Disraelian legacies and Tory populist sentiment designed to appeal to the new, predominantly working-class electorate. **[DOCUMENT V]** In an age of growing democracy, Churchill's apparent common touch and self-declared ability to interpret the people proved attractive to his more perplexed and anxious colleagues, and was a platform with which to appeal to the radical Liberals, led by Chamberlain, in pursuit of a progressive coalition of the centre. Alternatively, Salisbury pursued a more explicitly Tory and combative line, calculating that a Liberal exodus would occur naturally, given time for the artificial separations of party to realign with socio-economic realities. What Salisbury desired was an alliance of the 'possessing classes' working in defence of property and established institutions against the forces of spoliation and confiscation. Even though all three laboured towards the same goal, Northcote's style disillusioned followers and angered an increasingly restive Tory right, whilst Salisbury's and Churchill's approaches resonated with the bruised and frustrated sensitivities of the party in opposition.

Differences were also a product of the party's changing social constituency, with the slow decline of its rural basis and the emergence of a powerful provincial, middle-class, borough Conservatism. The strength of urban Tories by 1880 encouraged them to press their interests in the leadership, in particular to secure a more reformist Disraelian approach to policy in order to establish dominance over their mixed-class constituencies, and for a more vigorous style of leadership in place of Northcote's insipid direction. From 1881 urban Conservatives worked through local constituency associations and the National Union to advance these demands, enjoying the valuable patronage of Churchill, who perceived here a means of self-advancement and of damaging Northcote. The revolt of the suburbs lasted two years and eventually fizzled out in the summer of 1884, with the leadership still dominated by aristocrats and little having been obtained for the National Union beyond formal recognition and control of propaganda. What it did assist, however, was the advancement of both Salisbury and Churchill, who reached a working compact at the expense of the hapless Northcote. From early 1885, Salisbury was increasingly acknowledged as the principal Conservative leader and Churchill the de facto leader in the Commons.

However, divisions in the party and amongst the leaders were symptoms of a deeper anxiety: an acknowledgement, by the early 1880s, that future prospects for Tories looked exceedingly unfavourable. Many of the structural props to Conservative power in the country were steadily being eroded. Pressures in society and the economy undercut established beliefs and loosened customary social ties and obligations. [DOCUMENT VI] For example, reverence for the Established Church, the monarchy and traditional landed élites began to diminish under the combined attacks of Nonconformity, republicanism, socialism, the spread of new leisure and recreational opportunities and the expansion in educational provision following Forster's Education Act of 1870. Fluctuations in the trade cycle facilitated the growth of more aggressive trade unions, often associated with emergent socialist groups. The onset of cyclical unemployment provoked social unrest and prompted interest in welfare policies, a recognition that more traditional charitable and paternalistic methods of social control were no longer effective. This was primarily the result of falling incomes from land eroding aristocratic philanthropy. Falling returns on land also spread impoverishment and protest throughout rural areas. By the late 1870s, rural discontent was beginning to attract the attention of radical politicians sensitive to the rewards of aligning with this new social constituency. This fuelled pressure to enfranchise the agricultural labourers, which came in 1884, aiding the spread of nationalist sentiment, in the Celtic regions and especially Ireland, that posed a serious threat to the unity of the United Kingdom and the British empire.

At the heart of this disintegration of Conservative values and power lay the movement towards a democratic political system. With the electorate growing in size and independence, customary methods of political management being dismantled following the collapse of landed incomes, and the limits placed on election expenditure by the Corrupt Practices Act of 1883, Tories forecast difficulties. Few believed a natural Conservative majority existed amongst the new electorate. Instead, newly independent voters were more likely to be seduced by ambitious agitators and rabble-rousers, as the activities of the Irish Land League seemed to demonstrate. Increasing democracy would, therefore, entail a collapse in the party's electoral strength as the spectacular drop in support from county constituencies, once the bedrock of Tory power, seemed to show at the 1885 election. Although English county seats had increased from 170 to 231 as a consequence of the 1884–5 reform, the Tory share still fell from 120 seats in 1880 to just 99 in 1885, representing a decrease from 70 per cent to just 43 per cent of English county representation.

Democratic reforms also modified the composition of the electorate, moving it away from its propertied, educated, tax-paying, middle-class character of the mid-Victorian period, to an electorate where the un-propertied, the uneducated, the non-income-taxpayers, the have-nots predominated. This opened up several disturbing possibilities. One was that the new voters, lacking the benefits of property and swayed by the Socialist groups of the 1880s, would utilize their voting strength to advance their material interests at the expense of those with capital and property. The resulting pressure to redistribute wealth would expand the operations of the state and find demagogic and unscrupulous politicians only too happy to comply: witness Randolph Churchill's Dartford Programme and Joseph Chamberlain's Unauthorised Programme. Redistribution of wealth would also damage the existing social order, undermine Britain's commercial position, and endanger the empire by re-directing resources from imperial defence towards social welfare. Another anxiety was that democratic politics appeared to enhance the power of the government, a consequence of procedural changes during the 1880s that extended executive control over the parliamentary system, as well as introduce a new concept of the popular mandate. This unbalanced the constitution and curtailed checks upon a ministry, increasing the danger of an intrusive, appropriating government able to confiscate wealth and property at will (which was demonstrated for many Tories by Gladstone's Irish Land Act of 1881). If these were portents of the future, then politics and government were no longer a gentlemanly hobby but, as Salisbury saw it, a vicious struggle of life and death between the classes and the masses.

Collectively these problems of tactics, fraying party unity, leadership rivalries, the collapse of influence and the erosion of wider Conservative beliefs, helped to precipitate a second consecutive election defeat in 1885. Conservatives recouped just 12 extra seats on top of their 1880 total, amounting to 250 MPs, still 84 adrift of the Liberals (with 334 seats) and looking ominously like a return to their previous, almost permanent, minority party status. The result was all the more disappointing given that the election had followed Gladstone's accident-prone second ministry and that Parnell, leader of the Irish Nationalists, had recommended Irish support for Conservative candidates in Britain. From the vantage-point of 1885, Disraeli's election victory in 1874 looked more like a temporary blip than a new dawn for the party.

Reconstruction, 1885–1887

Despite failure at the 1885 election, several optimistic developments were discernible for Conservatives which, over the next two years, led to a major political reconstruction and a recovery in party fortunes. One was the vitality of middle-class, urban Conservatism which recorded, for the first time, the return of more villa than county Tory MPs. In England, for example, 114 urban Tory MPs were elected compared to 105 from the counties. In London, Tory seats rose from 36 per cent of the boroughs in 1880 to 60 per cent in 1885, winning thirty-five out of the fifty-nine available constituencies. These increases were repeated in various provincial city suburbs, such as Leeds, Sheffield and Liverpool. Indeed, so effective were boroughs at returning Tories that many of the landed élite deserted their uncertain county seats for suburban ones. Henry Chaplin, 'the farmers' friend', moved to Wimbledon and Walter Long left Wiltshire for the Strand.

The drift of urban, middle-class voters towards the Conservative party strengthened during the early 1880s, partly as a result of the growing radicalization of the Liberal party, the increased effectiveness of Tory constituency associations and, after 1883, the success of the Primrose League in organizing and educating increasing numbers of urban supporters. But alteration in the party's electoral base was primarily a consequence of the Redistribution Act of 1885 which Salisbury extracted from Gladstone in return for safe passage through the Lords of his Franchise Bill. At Salisbury's behest, the Act created new single-member constituencies defined along single interest or class lines. This ring-fenced the expanding middle-class suburbs of late-Victorian Britain, delivering at a stroke safe, class-segregated constituencies where Conservatives were 'high and dry on islands of their own': safe constituencies that compensated for the shrinkage in the county vote (J. P. Cornford, 'The transformation of Conservatism in the late nineteenth century', *Victorian Studies* 1963, 58). Single-member seats also destroyed the vital Liberal mechanism that had allowed Whigs and radicals to run in tandem. In future, local Liberal constituencies would have to choose between a Whig and a Radical candidate – a circumstance that kindled friction and hastened the Whigs' flight from the Liberal coalition.

As a by-product, the negotiations over redistribution confirmed Salisbury as overall party leader. Salisbury's direction of tactics and policy was critical at this point. He began to recognize the importance of the middle classes for the survival of the party and thus assisted their passage from Liberalism. In speeches he emphasized the threat to property posed by a Liberal government, pointing as evidence to the rising level of rates and taxation, and the close association of many progressive Liberals with the land reformer, Henry George, and the Land Nationalisation Society. In particular, he concentrated his fire on Chamberlain's brand of radical Liberalism and especially his 'Unauthorised Programme', a collection of ideas that included graduated taxation, the taxation of land values, compulsory purchase, smallholdings, free education and various schemes involving further state intervention. Through such attacks, Salisbury forged an alliance between urban and landed property-owners in a common defence of their wealth and privileges against an encroaching democracy.

Salisbury consolidated this alliance of property when Gladstone converted to Home Rule in December 1885. Instead of focusing his attack upon a measure of limited self-government for Ireland, Salisbury managed successfully to position Home Rule in a broader domestic and imperial context, representing it as a totem of all the subversive and destabilizing forces active in British society during the 1880s. Such tactics were framed to unite the conservatively-inclined around the Tory party. In Salisbury's hands, Home Rule came to symbolize servility in the face of the disintegrating movements of radicalism and socialism, the victory of lawlessness and the flouting of established authority, an undermining of property relations and the freedom of contract, disloyalty to the Crown and the constitution, religious intolerance and a threat to the unity of the United Kingdom and British empire. By playing up the bogey of the Irish threat, Salisbury re-energized traditional Conservative beliefs. Around this standard he assembled a broad and negative alliance of resistance, a union of those alarmed by the direction and pace of change in the late-Victorian period who were keen to preserve social order, the rule of law and the privileges of property, a strategy that proved its effectiveness at the election in July. Home Rule, then, became less a struggle over Ireland and more, in the words of Martin Pugh, a 'crucial battleground for the defence of British society' (M. Pugh, *The Tories and the People*, 89).

The second aspect of political reconstruction resulted from a strengthening of the Irish Nationalist party at the 1885 election. The rise from an irritating sixty-one MPs in 1880 to a strategically powerful eighty-six MPs thrust the Irish Question to the centre of British politics. Holding the balance in the Commons, the Irish were keen to barter for rewards, a factor that initially led Tories to co-operate with Parnell during Salisbury's six-month minority government of 1885. Some, such as Churchill, Lord Ashbourne and Lord Carnarvon, angled for a wider collaboration. But with Salisbury as leader little chance existed for the type of realignment Churchill had in mind, so Nationalists were forced back to their traditional allies the Liberals.

This was the situation when Gladstone, aware of the worsening social crisis in Ireland and the acute parliamentary arithmetic, converted to Home Rule in December 1885. By design or miscalculation, Gladstone's decision split the Liberal party, with ninety-three Liberal Unionists, led by Lord Hartington and Chamberlain, joining with the Tories to defeat the bill on its second reading in June. There was little, however, to suggest that the split would be permanent. Liberals regularly defected only to return to the fold once the immediate cause of secession had passed, as in 1866–7 and 1873–4. The Liberal Unionists, after all, regarded themselves as the true Liberals waiting for Gladstone to retire, not as turncoats or closet Tories finally outed by the realities of their position. Few would have relished co-operation with the reactionary Salisbury, though most would probably have shared Churchill's outlook, a consideration not lost on Salisbury himself.

Salisbury and Churchill realized that any political benefit could only come through a permanent breach. Churchill worked hard behind the scenes in an attempt to construct a centre party under Hartington based upon a compromise solution for Ireland. This, Churchill hoped, would attract support from non-Gladstonian Liberals and moderate Tories alike, but would exclude Salisbury. Not wanting to be sidelined by such a centrist coalition, Salisbury grabbed the initiative, swinging intemperately rightwards so as to polarize the murky political situation. In a speech to the National Union, he bitterly attacked Home Rule and suggested the Irish were incapable of self-government, comparing them to 'Hottentots' whose best option was twenty years of resolute British government. [DOCUMENT VII] The speech, as intended, outraged Liberal opinion and enthused Tories, widening the distance between them. If Liberal Unionists still hoped to return to the Liberal fold, then it was now a far wider gulf to bridge and one marked with such bitter recrimination that reconciliation would undoubtedly end the political careers of the mutineers. Salisbury, therefore, offered them political survival through an electoral pact: a joint Unionist platform with Liberal Unionists given a free run against Gladstonian candidates. For Liberal Unionists, the pact ensured the return of seventy-eight of their number at the July election. For Tories, a bloody election campaign fought between former comrades did much to consolidate the Liberal breach whilst Liberal Unionist candidates were limited to sitting MPs or to constituencies where Tories had no chance. The party also gained from a request by Hartington that anti-Home Rule Liberals should vote Conservative where no Liberal Unionist was standing, an invitation from a respected leader that may have mollified the conscience of many a disenchanted Liberal unhappy at Gladstone's step but uneasy about switching immediately to the Tory party.

The effectiveness of the Conservatives' electoral co-operation with Liberal Unionists was demonstrated at the 1886 election, when Gladstonians, although polling substantially more votes than Tories (1,241,000 to 1,038,000), collapsed massively in terms of seats. The Liberals retained just 191 seats, their lowest tally up to that point for the entire nineteenth century and a decline of 143 seats on their total of just eight months previously. On the other hand, Tories returned 316 MPs, some twenty short of an overall Commons majority, but with the seventy-eight Liberal Unionists enough to sustain a ministry as long as the alliance with (and between) Hartington and Chamberlain held. In other words, the electoral pact worked efficiently for both parties, and especially the Tories, by maximizing the anti-Gladstone vote. The election also registered a further movement of middle-class opinion to the Tory party, with a rise in English borough seats from 114 to 164 and in London a jump from thirty-five to forty-seven seats in 1886, triumphs that again augmented the strength of borough Conservatism in the party. The vigour of urban Toryism vindicated Salisbury's political tactics since 1884. Yet, somewhat ironically, the 1886 victory was also the product of a revival in the countryside. The counties that were thought all but lost after the 1885 result recovered some ground, with 174 English counties returning a Conservative MP, an advance from 43 per cent in 1885 to 72 per cent in 1886.

Conservatives in government, 1887–1900

The Conservative and Liberal Unionist parties dominated government for the next twenty years, apart from a brief and ineffectual Liberal interlude between 1892 and 1895. Their co-operation ensured continued electoral success, something that had eluded Tories since 1830. Yet for many years after 1886 both resisted fusion. Their first joint meeting was not held until 1892 and the formal entry of Liberal Unionists into Cabinet did not occur until 1895, some ten years after the Home Rule split. Indeed not until 1912 and the end of that electoral success, with three successive defeats, was full amalgamation achieved. Fusion was therefore a slow and far from inevitable outcome, and that made partnership difficult both between and within the two parties. Points of conflict affected the smooth working of the union: tensions that centred upon rival political strategies, problems of leadership and pressures on policy from the mix of new groups and interests, strains that nearly broke the alliance during the 1890 session.

Many Conservatives remained suspicious of their new allies, especially Chamberlain, and the likely price to be paid for their co-operation. The Tory right was a principal source of apprehension for the leadership, able to whip up party grumbles into serious disputes, as happened at Warwick and Leamington in 1892 over the forced withdrawal of Conservative candidates in favour of Liberal Unionist ones. On the other hand, Liberal Unionists were anxious to preserve their separate identity. This stemmed from their delicate constituency position which depended on appearing as anti-Gladstonian Liberals rather than surrogate Tories, whilst standing free from office rather than hamstrung by it meant that more could be extracted from the government. This was of particular concern to Chamberlain who needed to preserve his radical image if he were to retain popularity and secure his political duchy of Birmingham. **[DOCUMENT VIII]** This potential for instability encouraged certain leaders to search for ways to cement the relationship. The most significant attempt was one pursued by Churchill and Chamberlain, now in formal union, which looked to transform the alliance into a reformist, centre party along Palmerstonian lines and with a broad popular appeal. Collaboration was based on an agreed radical platform that included the provision of allotments and small-holdings, compulsory land transfer, free education, local government reform and a positive approach to Ireland and the empire.

Salisbury resisted these moves towards progressive Disraelian politics. Instead, he sought to keep the alliance upon the defensive and oppositional track he had established in 1885. In this he was inadvertently aided by Churchill himself who, in December 1886, resigned in a reckless attempt to force the issue – a move designed to wreck Salisbury's purely Tory government in order to reconstitute a broader Unionist cabinet under Hartington. The plan failed because Churchill badly miscalculated the temper of rank-and-file Conservatives, who were alarmed by the prospect of a Hartington-led coalition and perhaps weary of almost two years of political convulsion. He also misread the strength of Cabinet unity, for even his close ally, Hicks Beach, stayed temporarily loyal to the prime minister. Salisbury correctly predicted that Hartington would be unmoved by such gestures, given his mistrust of Churchill (who just months earlier had likened him to a boa constrictor) and his desire to maintain a separate party identity. To soothe possible Liberal Unionist consternation, however, he invited George Goschen, a Liberal Unionist with extensive contacts in the City, to be the chancellor of the Exchequer. Therefore, when Salisbury accepted Churchill's resignation there was no political reshuffle. Instead, to his great surprise, Churchill was consigned to the obscurity of the back benches.

Churchill's fall terminated manœuvres for a centrist fusion. The redirection of Unionism along a radical course would have to wait until Salisbury's retirement before it could again be canvassed, as Chamberlain attempted after 1903 with Tariff Reform. Yet, despite the relative tranquillity within the leadership, instability remained intrinsic to the Unionist alliance at both parliamentary level and amongst local constituencies and supporters. This was a result of its growing heterogeneity, caused by an expanding regional diversity, the assimilation of Liberal secessionists and the inward flow of middle-class support. [DOCUMENT IX] Such a broadening political, social and geographic base endowed Unionism with new values and created new economic interests to satisfy, whilst aggravating older views and interests. The struggle against Home Rule, for example, brought a more sectarian type of Irish Unionist into the alliance, predominantly sitting for an Ulster constituency and demanding more of an Orange tinge to Unionist Irish policy, a bias that often conflicted with moderate Liberal Unionist sentiments.

Of more importance, the influx of ex-Liberals reinforced an existing Conservative strain that mistrusted the state, as expressed through pressure groups like the Liberty and Property Defence League under Lord Wemyss. After 1886 anti-collectivist sentiment was more vigorously represented within Unionist circles, and espoused in the writings of A. V. Dicey and W. H. Mallock, than in its historic abode, the Liberal party. The allegiance of large sections of suburban and middle-class opinion to Unionism brought similar small-state, low-tax and low-rate sympathies and misgivings about the utility and cost of more 'progressive' initiatives associated with Disraeli, Churchill and Chamberlain. With suburban Conservatives these sentiments translated into intense activity at municipal level, often in concert with the Primrose League, to wrest control of local boards and councils from profligate radicals. Such activity proved successful and gave Conservatives local bridgeheads of influence. They also pressurized the government to reduce their local rate levels, pressure which Salisbury's chancellors of the exchequer, Goschen and, from 1895 to 1902, Hicks Beach, mollified with rising amounts of central funds in the form of grants-in-aid.

Conflicting with these attitudes were the more statist elements of the alliance. These included older Tory sections, whose authoritarian and paternalistic instincts had never flinched from a strong state and government intervention, and who were hostile to a more libertarian and *laissez-faire* outlook. Of more impact was the enlarged Unionist presence in manufacturing and agricultural constituencies adversely affected by depression or intense foreign competition. In these regions Unionists insisted on a number of positive and active responses from central government: the relief of rates, currency reform (including bimetallism), the alleviation of acute poverty and unemployment through housing reform, allotments and small-holdings, public health improvements, public works programmes and even old-age pensions. [DOCUMENT VIII] This collection of anxieties and demands converged into the Fair Trade movement, a precursor of the Tariff Reform League, which, throughout the 1880s and 1890s pressed for tariff barriers to limit foreign imports in order to secure domestic employment and sustain profit margins. The movement attracted much support from the National Union, from back-bench Tories, and inevitably, from Churchill, scenting another possible ladder to climb by. Fair Trade united sections of capital and agriculture in a common defence of their interests through the introduction of tariffs, in a similar fashion to the cause of the Union. It also stimulated and overlapped with an interest in empire, where soft and protected markets might offer stable levels of production to manufacturers and opportunities for emigration to ease unemployment in British cities. Already then, by the 1880s and 1890s some Unionists were beginning to move in Social Imperialist directions, making a common association between the state, tariffs, empire and social welfare. Thus, the heterogeneity of Unionism added numerous points of stress and fracture: with progressive *versus* traditionalist; collectivist *versus* free-trader: aristocrat *versus* middle class *versus* working class, and urban *versus* rural.

If the potential for internal disharmony was increased after 1886, then so was the vulnerability of the Unionist alliance to Liberal assaults, and particularly to traditional attacks against Tory landlordism. This lay in the switch of allegiance made by many Liberal peers as a consequence of Gladstone's conversion to Home Rule. It created a severe imbalance in the House of Lords, evident when the Lords rejected the second Home Rule bill in 1894 by 419 to 41, the largest majority in its entire history. This action left the House susceptible to a Liberal attack on a 'Peers' versus the 'People' platform. Both Gladstone and Rosebery, his replacement as prime minister in 1894, intended launching such a campaign, something which Salisbury took great care to avoid by selecting mostly unpopular bills for rejection. The swift collapse of the Liberal ministry in 1895 probably cut short this stratagem although its feasibility remained, especially if Unionists were ever to over-employ the veto or stray into less obviously unpopular legislation. On the other hand, it did provide Unionists with a ready tool to curb or 'check' radical Liberal legislation from the Commons, as happened with Gladstone's Employers' Liability Bill of 1893. Salisbury, as leader in the Lords for this period, justified this purpose by his referendal theory which contended the Lords' absolute right to veto bills not submitted to the people via an election or referendum. In practice it was an ill-disguised method of neutering a Liberal government and reinforcing Salisbury's innate defensive instincts. It also preserved for the Unionist alliance, when in opposition, a controlling hand on the levers of state.

Yet the Unionist alliance was rarely in opposition during these years. Of the four general elections between 1886 and 1900 Unionists won three and averaged 315 seats, which compared favourably with the one victory at the four elections preceding 1886, and the subsequent loss of three elections in succession after 1900. Here was the essential cement of the Unionist alliance: an underlying electoral vitality, the continuation of which depended on maintaining separate identities and marginalizing those tensions which periodically tormented it. Beyond this, the Unionist alliance worked smoothly enough. Outside the heady world of Westminster, the alliance operated efficiently at constituency level as a powerful and energetic instrument of electoral management under the skilful guidance of Captain Middleton. Salisbury had long recognized the benefits of party organization. He rued the fact that an extra 2,000 votes strategically placed would have avoided defeat in 1880 and again in 1892. For him organization was a vital means to supervise democracy and to marshal and channel an increasingly rootless electorate. Congenial relations between Unionist leaders also owed much to Lord Wolmer, the Liberal Unionist chief whip and Salisbury's son-in-law. On the Tory side, W. H. Smith and then Balfour, as leaders of the Commons, and Akers-Douglas, the chief whip, were all well practised in the back-room art of persuasion and committed to the success of the enterprise. Balfour especially played a leading role in managing Chamberlain by providing a direct channel to Salisbury.

A common desire to remain flexible helped to underpin working relations. Goschen and Hartington proved surprisingly conservative, Smith was well-respected, Balfour was pliant and sympathetic and Chamberlain was realist enough to temper his radicalism. Less obviously flexible was Salisbury. What reforms he allowed through were either emasculated, as with the Workmen's Compensation Act of 1897, or innocuous to the interests he served, as with housing reforms, or they simply recognized an altered and irreversible situation, as with the creation of county councils in 1888 and the Irish Local Government Act of 1898. Yet even Salisbury saw the importance of compromise and generally allowed ministers freedom of operation. Disagreement, however, was never far from the surface, particularly on questions of social reform and Church affairs, which made it doubly fortuitous that imperial and foreign policy issues figured prominently in politics during the 1890s. Clearly Chamberlain felt the pull of such considerations in rejecting the Home Office and the Exchequer for the Colonial Office when he entered the government in 1895. They were also areas in which Salisbury won general acclaim and tended to unite rather than divide the alliance.

Ultimately, the electoral strength of the alliance lay in its ability to project an assortment of successful and attractive images: a composite appeal that connected a diverse and sometimes conflicting assemblage of political supporters to Unionism, facilitated by various media, such as growing Conservative contact with the press and the many societies and leagues of this period. Part of the appeal of Unionism was a revived Palmerstonian image of a broad-based centrist coalition combining defence of British interests abroad with a mildly reformist policy at home. The figure of Lord Hartington and the scraps of legislation allowed through by Salisbury substantiated this representation, which proved attractive to centre-ground, non-partisan and floating opinion. Another part of the appeal, associated with Chamberlain from 1892 onwards when he replaced Hartington as leader of the Liberal Unionists in the Commons, was radical Unionism. This drew upon a Disraelian legacy, the Tory Democracy of Churchill and Chamberlain's own experience of progressive municipal government in Birmingham. Chamberlain championed a constructive programme of reforms aimed at appeasing the working classes through social and economic amelioration, thus drawing them from the lure of socialism and, at the same time, securing middle-class interests. **[DOCUMENT VIII]** During the 1890s much of the ministry's reformist legislation, such as the Education Act of 1891 and the Workmen's Compensation Act, was put down to Chamberlain, a dubious claim for he clearly lacked the influence to drive pensions through. Ironically, Chamberlain's attempt to mobilize the resources of the state and the empire in order to achieve his constructive Unionism enticed the more paternalistic and authoritarian, far-right Tories into collaboration with him.

However, by far the most dominant appeal in Unionism was the 'protective and defensive' Toryism that Salisbury had constructed during the political turmoil of 1885–6 (A. L. Kennedy, *Salisbury 1830–1903: Portrait of a Statesman*, 193). This centred on a reverence for social order, freedom of contract, inviolable property rights, an educated élite, social privileges, established authority and the empire, alongside older shibboleths – the Crown, the Church, the nation and the constitution – which were re-invigorated by the hostile environment of the 1880s to become widely approved symbols of the status quo. Here was an appeal that united a swathe of different interests: agricultural concerns, attracted by a historic bond and, more tangibly, by active assistance in the form of rating relief in 1896; suburban middle classes, attracted by the low-tax policies and financial rectitude of Salisbury's chancellors; employers and factory owners, fearful of the rise of trade unionism, mollified by a vigorous upholding of social authority and the suppression of labour unrest through the law courts and even, on occasions, by the deployment of cavalry; and lastly, the expanding lower middle classes, similarly fearful of the masses, placated by the firm maintenance of social hierarchy as well as the promotion of imperial grandeur. This re-invigorated Toryism proved a particularly successful recipe for the Primrose League, especially among the lower middle class whose acute status-consciousness was nicely satiated by the League's mock medieval garb and its emphasis on deference and hierarchy.

In addition, Salisburian Toryism appealed to certain sections of the working class. Popular Toryism had a long ancestry dating back to the Volunteer movement and the Church-and-King demonstrations of the French Revolutionary period, sentiments still to be found in the 1880s in certain regions and communities. It represented a more guttural Toryism with a reverence for 'Throne and Altar' that reinforced a vigorous constitutionalism. It also drew upon a chauvinistic patriotism, especially strong in areas of high immigration and religious friction such as Lancashire, with its Irish community, and the East End of London, with its European refugees. Another component was a robust support for empire and the defence of British interests abroad, a consequence of many industries being adversely affected by foreign competition (such as the metalworks of Birmingham, Sheffield and Wolverhampton) or family connections with the military or naval services, or of work in shore-based support operations such as ports, depots, dockyards, arsenals and armaments factories. Popular Toryism could also draw on a pessimistic working-class culture. This included an acceptance of the way things were, a deference for social betters from whom this class might receive charity, and a libertarian self-reliance that echoed the growing anti-collectivist stance of the Tory party; and it was reflected in an indulgence in drink and hedonistic entertainment, free from the interference of 'do-gooding', Nonconformist Liberals (for the drink trade was a powerful Tory interest group). Salisburian Toryism was able to cast its net widely.

A precarious dominance?

Yet, although Conservatives were in government for almost twenty years, their hold on power was much more fragile than such tenure suggests. All three of their election victories between 1886 and 1900 occurred under slightly anomalous and exceptional circumstances. They were timed to coincide with the harvest or periods of intense manufacturing activity, so as to keep potentially hostile voters away from the polling stations. Both the 1886 and 1895 elections were scheduled at moments when the Liberal leadership was badly split; whilst the 1900 election was called during the South African war on the crest of a patriotic wave of sentiment. Because of these unusual conditions, Liberal candidatures collapsed, prompting a rise in uncontested seats (225 in 1886, 189 in 1895 and 243 in 1900). Conservative victories were therefore won on a restricted Liberal vote rather than by an increase in Unionist support and have an aberrant quality: they hide the underlying strength of the Liberal vote, along with a growing alignment of Labour with Liberalism. At only one election, in 1895, did the Conservatives win a clear majority of seats over all other parties: they thus remained throughout the late nineteenth century heavily dependent on Irish and Liberal Unionist support. In particular, the ability of Liberal Unionism to offer a renewed Palmerstonian image and to attract enough centrist, moderate opinion was critical to the survival of predominantly Conservative governments, given that British elections were, and still are, won primarily at the centre. In this they were assisted by the radicalization of the Liberal party after 1886. Most periods of Conservative domination, 1807–27, 1886–1905, 1924–40, 1951–64 and since 1979, have been sustained by an opposition vulnerable to accusations of extremism and disloyalty and easily portrayed as a threat to property – a characterization made easier by Gladstone's decision to continue as party leader. To be able to depict Gladstone as the increasingly senile and slightly unhinged radical leader was invaluable to Unionists. At the same time, the presence of Gladstone prevented the return of Hartington or Chamberlain because it kept alive Home Rule and all the personal bitterness that surrounded the split of 1886. 'Mr Gladstone's existence', Lord Salisbury commented, 'was the greatest source of strength which the Conservative party possessed'. Tories, therefore, were able to dominate government more by default than by any substantial increase in their support. Though slightly diluted, late nineteenth-century Britain remained essentially liberal in its political and cultural leanings.

Of more significance, the Conservative party encountered a collection of injurious and largely unsolvable structural pressures.

Salisbury's great strength had been his prudent management of all the conflicting interests and ambitions within the Unionist alliance: the industrialist against agriculturalist; collectivists against free-traders, old-fashioned authoritarian Tories against Conservative democrats; and radical Unionism against negative Toryism. He balanced these diverse interests by adopting a common defensive, property-based posture. However, by the late 1890s Salisbury's direction began to falter – a consequence of illness and a growing preoccupation with foreign affairs, combined with acute strains in the economy and society that destabilized the delicate equilibrium of Unionism. At the heart of these pressures lay rising levels of government expenditure, a result of the incremental growth of state responsibilities as well as of rising costs of imperial defence. As expenditure outpaced government revenue, there arose an intense pressure to raise taxation or cut government costs. This presented political quandaries which Salisbury could only suppress or delay. For example, an increase in taxes would threaten the wealth of urban middle-class supporters and endanger vital economic interests, such as the competitiveness of British exports and the City of London. On the other hand, cutting government expenditure would mean shaving the military budget at a time of rising international tension and expanding imperial commitments. It would also mean restricting social legislation, such as old-age pensions, at a time when independent working-class political organization was becoming increasingly evident and more working-class voters were coming onto electoral registers – in 1885 the electorate was 5.7 million, by 1910 it was nearly eight million – considerations that lay behind Chamberlain's increased restlessness by 1900 and the growing attraction of radical Unionism. Limiting expenditure would also hit Tory support in the counties by reducing rate relief or grants-in-aid for agricultural interests. Whichever way Salisbury turned, by the end of the century it appeared that his limited, well-balanced, property-based, low-tax, low-temperature 'quietist' brand of Conservatism could not survive much longer (E. Green, *The Crisis of Conservatism*, 125–35).

4. The Conservative Party in Crisis, 1900–1914

Slippage, 1900–1905

Salisbury's defensive coalition of property-owners that had sustained the fragile political dominance of Unionists since 1886, began to unravel after the 1900 general election. Although victorious in 1900, with 334 Conservatives and sixty-eight Liberal Unionists returned, the result hid an underlying vulnerability. This was the product of various developments. Salisbury's loss of political grip, and his subsequent retirement in July 1902, created divisions within the leadership. The death of that inveterate old Tory, Queen Victoria, in 1901 was followed by the accession of the less partisan Edward VII. As the executive strengthened its hold over Parliament, constitutional tensions grew. Increased rivalry between the great powers channelled more resources to imperial defence and fuelled unease about Britain's military competence. A perception of decline in Britain's economic and commercial situation prompted some to question established free-trade economic orthodoxy. A growing popular awareness of poverty by the 1890s led to mounting demands for the state to alleviate the problem. And as state responsibilities grew, the fiscal and expenditure position worsened: 'The nation appeared to have its neck in a gradually tightening noose from which no easy escape was possible' (A. Freidberg, *The Weary Titan*, 103). All these anxieties and strains were amplified by the South African war (1899–1902) into a major crisis of party and state.

The war initiated the largest mobilization of military personnel since the Crimean war: 364,000 men from Britain and a further 80,000 troops from the colonies at a cost to the British tax-payer of a massive £200 million. The rise in government expenditure necessitated an increase in the level of taxation from 9 per cent of the gross national product in 1890 to 15 per cent in 1900. Conservative anxieties about a large, interfering and confiscatory state were beginning to materialize – but they were a consequence of their own party's initiatives rather than those of extravagant radical politicians. In political terms these circumstances had a significant impact on the party's support and appeal. Rising taxation and government expenditure undermined the Conservatives' low-tax, small-state and financially prudent image which had proved so successful in winning over business and commercial interests and in constructing suburban enclaves of middle-class support. Furthermore, requiring three years and all the resources of the world's largest imperial power to defeat a scratch army of farmers severely dented their self-promotion as the party of empire, of patriotic sentiment and national pride. This undermined popular confidence in their stewardship of the empire, a situation aggravated by the ensuing diplomatic isolation which Britain faced from 1900 and revelations about 'methods of barbarism' in imperial management in the shape of concentration camps and Chinese slave-labour. A smack of authoritarian Conservatism unnerved an essentially liberal British public opinion.

In addition, the war generated anxiety at the physical condition of Britain's working population, after a third of the volunteers were rejected as unfit for service on medical grounds. This diverted popular attention away from imperial issues and towards a growing debate about domestic welfare provision. Social reform had never been a high priority for most Conservatives, despite Disraelian and Churchillian myths to the contrary. It was especially distasteful to anti-collectivist sections of the party. Developments after 1902 reinforced these inclinations as government was forced to re-balance national finances by severe cuts in state expenditure. The rigid ceilings on taxation, necessitated by their middle-class electorate, constrained the Conservatives' room for manœuvre. However, welfare provision was now perceived as a pressing issue as the threat of independent working-class politics was realized in 1900 with the creation of the Labour Representation Committee. A more progressive, welfarist brand of Liberalism also gained influence in the upper circles of the Liberal party, in recognition of its increasing electoral reliance upon working-class votes. In the area of social policy, then, Unionists appeared financially and electorally hand-tied and were thus easily outpaced by their opponents.

Taken together, the damaging effects of the war, with its logistical shortcomings, military reverses, financial overspend and poor condition of recruits, fostered wider questions about the health of the British state. Queries were raised about the well-being of the governmental and political system, the role and function of the state, the effectiveness of the educational structure and the future management of the empire. These questions stimulated a general climate of renewal and revitalization across the parties which became concentrated in various national efficiency groupings. Salisburian Conservatism could not respond to this spirit of rejuvenation, given its foundation upon a defensive instinct and the preservation of state institutions as bastions of the existing order. Whereas Salisbury's representation of Unionism had chimed with (and, indeed, helped to construct) the political context of the mid-1880s, by the early 1900s, in a new political climate, it seemed antiquated, indifferent and negative. This was reflected in a succession of by-election defeats from 1901 onwards and in the rise of various leagues and societies dedicated to furthering traditional conservative issues (military and naval supremacy, imperial unity, economic security) largely because the party was no longer seen as the most effective prospect (F. Coetzee, *For Party and Country*).

As Salisbury's defensive alliance lost political appeal and electoral purchase, so alternative Conservative strategies emerged that were better equipped to respond to the new challenges. The most overlooked and underrated of these was the strategy devised by Arthur Balfour, Salisbury's successor as prime minister. Balfour never wholly shared his uncle's ideological negativism, a consequence of his pivotal role in co-ordinating action with Liberal Unionists and, in particular, with Chamberlain. With Salisbury safely retired, Balfour revived a more centrist, Conservative legacy: a combination of 'Tory men and Whig measures' that attempted to balance the party's traditional support for defence and security with practical measures of reform to restore public credibility and financial rectitude, to reverse thereby the party's flagging political fortunes. During his premiership an impressive number of reforms were enacted, some, such as the Education Act of 1902, which created an integrated national education system, the result of his direct supervision. In domestic affairs plans were laid for an Unemployed Assistance Board and an Aliens Act was finally introduced in 1905. Both were attempts to address the issue of welfare by tackling unemployment, measures that also retreated from clear free-trade principles. In military administration, economies were pushed through and a Committee of Imperial Defence was established by the time the Tories left office in 1905, although more far-reaching army reform proved elusive, much to Balfour's annoyance. In foreign affairs, Britain's isolation was alleviated by an Anglo-Japanese alliance in 1902 and the Anglo-French entente in 1904, agreements which allowed the Admiralty to economize by rationalizing naval commitments. Moreover, initiatives to buy out the Anglo-Irish landlords were extended by the Wyndham Land Act of 1903 and tentative moves towards devolved government for Ireland were attempted, albeit unsuccessfully.

Balfour's mild, reformist approach sought to maintain established party interests, especially those of landowners, commercial and financial groups and middle-class sectors, whilst pushing through essential policies for stabilizing the financial system after the South African war. It was a calm, sensible and practical strategy, perhaps even an exercise in damage limitation, and thus not one necessarily formulated to win the 1905–6 election. Its purpose was to avoid more extreme strategies, maintain unity and preserve as much support as possible while the party waited for the political pendulum to swing back in its favour. However, the strategy did not enthuse party supporters or back-bench MPs, least of all those sitting for marginal constituencies. Moreover, it confirmed the appearance of hesitancy and indolence suggested by the leadership's failure to legislate in certain key areas, notably old-age pensions. Such apparent defects left it vulnerable to the more radical and activist brand of Unionism championed by Chamberlain. This strand challenged Balfour's mild approach between 1903 and 1905 and then, in the wake of the election disaster, dominated it thereafter.

At the heart of this activist brand of Unionism was Chamberlain's policy of tariff reform, launched in a dramatic speech at Birmingham on 15 May 1903 which Leo Amery described 'as direct and provocative as the theses which Luther nailed to the Church door at Wittenberg' (L. Amery, *My Political Life*, 236). Chamberlain viewed tariff reform as a panacea for the assortment of financial, social and political problems confronting the country by the early 1900s. **[DOCUMENT X]** It was a mechanism for eliminating economic depression and avoiding longer-term decline. Protecting British markets, both industrial and agricultural, with trade barriers would mean a less severe business cycle, and so securing returns from land, maintaining profit margins and stable levels of employment through a unity of capital and labour in a producers' alliance. The money raised from tariffs would be used to finance social policies. This, along with greater job security, thought Chamberlain and others, would be a sufficiently seductive package to undercut the appeal of the new Labour party and swing growing numbers of working-class voters behind Unionism. In addition, granting imperial territories exemption from tariffs would establish a free-trade area, an imperial *zollverein*, that would diminish the likelihood of imperial disintegration and, instead, strengthen the cultural and political bonds of empire via closer economic ties.

As with Salisbury's strong anti-Home Rule stance in the mid-1880s, tariff reform seemed to respond to, and reflect, the contemporary political context. It could also draw upon a number of deeper Conservative traditions and instincts to construct a wide base of support in the party and the country. It fell upon well-prepared ground, echoing the arguments of the Fair Trade League of the 1880s and 1890s, and thus receiving support from depressed industrialists and hard-hit agricultural labourers, farmers and landowners. It appropriated the Disraelian image of empire, national pride and social reform (and was similarly used to target working-class communities) and aligned with the crusading spirit and activism of Churchill. It even exhibited strong parallels with Salisbury's defensive Conservatism, aiming to preserve the rights and privileges of property and appealing to middle-class sections by shifting the burden of taxation onto an indirect basis, thus avoiding the more progressive, direct schemes then being voiced by some Liberal and Labour activists. Tariff reform also enlisted Salisbury's faith in the power of the state to maintain social order and the authority of established political élites – although Chamberlain argued that state action be exercised in the economic sphere and not be applied, as in Salisbury's case, through a vigorous defence of the law and legal process. Even so, a sufficient streak of authoritarianism still remained to extend tariff reform's appeal to Tories of a more traditional or extreme right outlook.

In short, tariff reform offered solutions to a number of serious electoral and financial dilemmas facing the party. It embraced many basic Conservative priorities, such as the protection of property, defence of the existing social order and imperial security, and was not simply a Liberal Unionist plot foisted on the party. Nor was it something overly ideological and activist, alien to true Conservatism: it could be set firmly in the pantheon of Conservative traditions and myths. Yet, despite its potential, Chamberlain was never able comprehensively to stamp tariff reform on the party in the same way that Salisbury had done with anti-Home Rule. Certainly,

Chamberlain won over a majority in the parliamentary party and the constituencies to his policy, especially between 1907 and 1910. But the policy never took root during the Edwardian period and could therefore be deferred by Balfour in 1911 and emasculated at the end of 1912 by Bonar Law, himself once a leading tariff reformer. To some extent this was a reflection of personalities. Salisbury had background and breeding and had always been a Tory, whilst Chamberlain, a screw manufacturer and radical Liberal Unionist, was never quite 'one of us'. Chamberlain also faced dogged opponents throughout his campaign, in the shape of Balfour and the duke of Devonshire (Lord Hartington until 1891). Salisbury, on the other hand, had enjoyed a relatively clear field after 1886, when the erratic Churchill effectively self-destructed.

Tariff reform also suffered from several structural difficulties. Not all industrial and commercial interests welcomed the raising of tariff barriers. Certainly the depressed iron and steel trades of Sheffield and Birmingham and farming interests, hit by cheap Canadian corn and the refrigerated carriage of meats, looked longingly at protection of the home market. But successful export-orientated sectors, such as the Lancashire cotton mills, saw tariffs as regressive, liable to raise the price on incoming raw materials and expose their trade to retaliatory action abroad. The financial sector, based in the City of London and a major political prop of the Conservative party, could similarly perceive little benefit for their business. Quite simply, the British economy was too heterogeneous for the imposition of a blanket tariff to benefit all. Tariff reformers therefore struggled to find the right balance among the industrial and commercial interests. In 1904 they instituted a Tariff Commission of fifty-nine leading experts to search for a 'scientific' tariff. Instead, the commission reinforced opinion that the British economy was anatomically resistant to the type of tariff walls that Chamberlain saw being erected in Germany, France and the USA.

More direct political damage resulted from the necessity of placing duties on incoming raw materials. First, raw materials included food stuffs, which had to be included if tariffs were to be of value to agricultural interests, but duties on foodstuffs exposed tariff reform to the cry of 'dear food', a damaging rebuff with injurious electoral consequences in working-class constituencies. It also raised once again perceptions, put to rest in the 1840s, that Tories sought to use the state as an instrument for their own class interests. Ironically Chamberlain, in looking to use tariff reform to forge a cross-class, producers' alliance, may have incited class awareness and friction instead. Second, taxing incoming raw materials contradicted tariff reform's imperial dimension, because the main imperial exports to Britain were raw materials and agricultural goods. Nor would the colonies lightly discard protection of their own fledgeling industries for fear of being undercut by Britain's industrial might. So it is clear that a number of incongruities lay at the heart of the tariff policy.

Because of these inconsistencies, tariff reform was unable to convert everyone in the Unionist alliance. A determined anti-state, free-trade element resisted Chamberlain's strategy, a group highly placed in leadership circles and including Goschen, Hicks Beach, Ritchie (all Unionist chancellors of the Exchequer since 1886), the duke of Devonshire, Hugh and Robert Cecil, the sons of Lord Salisbury, and Winston Churchill, Randolph's son, who joined the Liberals within a year of Chamberlain's announcement. The obstinacy of these Unionist 'free-fooders' ensured a period of intense party conflict, fought out at constituency level where tariff reformers, through their Confederate movement, tried to unseat known 'free-fooders'. From 1903 onwards the Unionist alliance was in a state of civil war.

It was the fillip which tariff reform gave to the Liberal party that was perhaps its greatest shortcoming. Liberals unified in defence of the Holy Grail of their political and economic vision, free trade. They now enjoyed a clear platform from which to attack the Tories, with arguments as familiar as stories from the Bible which could reunite the wider liberal coalition in the country, and so end their self-imposed late-Victorian abstention. (We might also include Liberal anger towards the 1902 Education Act, the tweaking of another traditional Liberal tenet that united the party.) Free trade was also common ground that helped to cement the electoral alliance between Liberals and the Labour party, as agreed by Herbert Gladstone and MacDonald in 1903; this alliance maximized the anti-Unionist vote and prevented Conservatives holding office again for the remainder of the pre-war period.

These various issues lay behind Balfour's reluctance firmly to endorse tariff reform, and his championing of a sort of half-way, retaliatory stance as a means to unify the party whilst continuing with his milder, liberal Conservative strategy. But this simply confused matters. Instead of plumping for one approach, he bestrode two different lines, denying the party clear direction and purpose and presenting the country with a confused choice. The Unionist alliance thus slid towards electoral disaster, a fate that even clever eleventh-hour tactics, designed by Balfour to reopen Liberal wounds, could not avert.

Defeat and opposition, 1906–1909

Few observers were surprised when the Unionist party lost the 1906 general election. On top of divisions over strategy and bitterness arising from the tariff issue, the alliance had a staleness about it as it entered the polls in December 1905. Balfour was widely criticized as remote, content to surround himself with relatives (the cousinhood), whilst remaining distant from the populace. Such an image had worked for Salisbury, whose calmness and detachment appeared almost reassuring in the threatening political atmosphere of the 1880s. By 1905 it hung badly on Balfour. But what observers were perhaps not prepared for was the scale of the Liberal victory, rising from 184 seats in 1900 to 401 in 1906 and reducing the Unionists from 402 to a mere 156 seats, with some notable casualties including Balfour himself. The party lost crucial support in Lancashire and London, particularly in working-class constituencies which were won over to the Liberal–Labour alliance and stayed loyal to it in 1910. The defeat was the biggest in its history and initiated the Unionists' longest continuous period in opposition. Not until 1915 did the Tories again attain office and not with a Commons' majority until October 1922.

On the other hand, what is most revealing about the election statistics is the relative stability of the Unionist vote across the whole period from 1880 to 1906. The vote in 1906 was just 3.4 per cent below the 1892 result, but they were 158 seats worse off. They collected exactly the same percentage of the vote as in 1885, 43.6 per cent, yet won nearly 100 fewer seats. If the Unionist vote was relatively stable, despite the varying number of seats captured, late-Victorian and early Edwardian elections were clearly being decided elsewhere, particularly in the fluctuating numbers of Liberal voters and the party's co-operation with Labour. The Liberal poll, for example, appeared to fluctuate in direct relation to the number of uncontested seats. The 1906 election saw a fall in their number, from 243 in 1900 to 114 in 1906, allowing the party to garner more support at the same moment as Liberal voters, inspired by the attack on free trade and education, moved away from abstention. The alliance with Labour similarly undercut the Unionist electoral position by avoiding three-cornered contests which had previously split the progressive vote, thus maximizing the anti-Unionist vote in the same way that the Conservative–Liberal Unionist alliance had previously maximized the anti-Gladstone vote.

This was of small comfort to the Unionist rump that limped back to Westminster to take its place in a Commons chamber where three-quarters of the occupants sneered at and derided its members. 'The house is a strange place just now', A. Forster commented to the future Conservative leader, Bonar Law. The painful adjustment to opposition, after nearly twenty continuous years in office, was made worse by the realization that the Labour party had grown from two seats at the 1900 election to nearly thirty seats five years later, sweeping traditional working-class Tory constituencies, such as those in Lancashire, out of Tory hands for the first time. **[DOCUMENT XI]** It was also galling that the fortunes of the empire now lay with Liberal ministers, many of whom had been pro-Boer during the war and were closely associated with the anti-imperialist Labour and Irish Nationalist parties. Moreover, the powers of government and the state had grown massively since the last period of Liberal majority government in 1885. The potential for harm and interference by a radical government was far greater. For many Unionists, it seemed as if the Salisburian nightmare of radical ministers vying for the votes of the property-less by appropriating the wealth of the rich was coming true.

These anxieties multiplied throughout the party, fuelling a growing sense of despair about the future and desperation for tougher methods to protect property and established society from a radical Liberal government. This apprehension was held temporarily in check by Chamberlain's tariff reform campaign which gained in popularity inside the party after 1906. Indeed, the events of 1906 seemed to endorse Chamberlain's more apocalyptic vision of the future. Party anxieties were also mollified by the House of Lords, which became the focus of Unionist activity, as it had done in the 1892–5 Parliament; Unionists were assured of an inbuilt majority that might still 'control, whether in power or opposition, the destinies of this great Empire' (D. Dutton, *His Majesty's Loyal Opposition*, 69). Throughout the 1906–10 Parliament, Lord Lansdowne, the Unionist leader in the Lords, deftly pruned Liberal legislation under Balfour's careful guidance, ensuring that sectional and unpopular bills like the Education Bill of 1906 and the Licensing Bill of 1908 were mauled, whilst allowing more obviously sensitive legislation, such as the Trades Disputes Bill of 1906, to proceed. It may be that the Lords were simply performing their assigned constitutional role, and were in any case willing to compromise upon most of the bills they amended. Yet the fact remains that when targeted carefully, the Lords' powers of veto were a useful weapon for the Unionists and, up until 1909, enabled them, with some success, to portray the Liberal government as ineffective and pandering to its own sectionalist interests.

On the other hand, though shrunken, the Conservative parliamentary party was now more unified. 'Free-fooders' had fallen disproportionately in 1906, with the majority of those MPs returning being adherents of the full tariff policy. This encouraged Balfour to reposition himself in order to remain leader, snuggling closer to Chamberlain with the 'Valentine' exchange of letters in February 1906 and, then, in a speech at Hull early in 1907. For the first time since 1903, the party was relatively free of internal strife and enjoyed a degree of cohesion on tariff reform. This position gained credibility with the downturn in the trade cycle during 1907–8 which enhanced the appeal of tariffs as an alternative to the failing free-trade system. The election of 1906 also emptied the party of much dead wood. A depleted parliamentary presence enabled young men with talent to advance quickly in the party hierarchy, notably Austen Chamberlain, F. E. Smith and Bonar Law; this had been impeded before 1905 by Balfour's nepotism.

Revolution, 1909–1911

The mixed political fortunes of the party after 1906 turned sharply against the Unionists from 1909, as many of the props that sustained the existing social order, including the empire, the landed interest and the constitution, came under attack from a Liberal government. At the heart of this change lay a revitalization of the Liberal party, which shifted in a more radical direction as a consequence of Asquith's replacing of Campbell-Bannerman as prime minister in 1908, Lloyd George's appointment to the Exchequer and, to a lesser extent, Winston Churchill's appearance at the Board of Trade. The Asquith–Lloyd George alliance was pivotal in the new ministry, which combined traditional liberal objectives with New Liberal concerns in what proved to be one of the most dynamic, reforming governments of the twentieth century.

The origins of this radicalization lay in the Liberals' ability to break free of nineteenth-century financial restraints and circumvent the taxation/electoral nexus that curbed government extravagance. Previously, governments had found that raising taxation to pay off national debts or fund social policies would undermine their electoral position, given the close correlation between taxation and the franchise. By the early 1900s this correlation was no longer as close, following the extension of the franchise to non-tax-paying, working-class groups. Hence, the previous discipline whereby tax rises were counterbalanced by electoral protest no longer applied. As Liberals moved into closer alliance with Labour, and the shrinkage in their middle-class vote was compensated by an increase in working-class support, so the logic and opportunities of this new situation channelled upwards to the leadership. These political considerations encouraged Asquith in 1907, and then Lloyd George in 1909, who was desperate to find extra resources to fund pensions and naval rearmament, to move towards a new tax system based on graduation (that is, tax bands) and differentiation (that is, taxing unearned income, such as land, rather than earned income, such as capital). This disproportionately targeted the landed classes and super-rich, who held the largest amount of unearned income and were unlikely to vote Liberal; thus permitting the raising of revenue without impairing the Liberals' electoral support. For the Liberal government this situation opened up a whole range of reformist possibilities. For Unionists the spectre of the radical, appropriating government, for so long a part of Unionist demonology, had finally appeared.

Unionist resistance to these financial innovations centred on Lloyd George's budget of April 1909, the 'People's budget', which increased death duties, imposed higher rates on unearned income, increased inheritance duties, introduced super-tax on incomes over £5,000, and modest taxes on land. In themselves they followed precedents set by Sir William Harcourt in 1894 and, more radically, by Asquith in 1907. In retrospect, they were exceptionally mild. However, for Unionists the budget represented a series of grave threats. It was a further attack on private property that extended the principle of redistribution. It was also thought to have subverted the constitution by smuggling in social reforms under the shelter of a finance bill, which it was assumed the Lords would never dare veto.

Yet if allowed through by the Lords, it could set a dangerous precedent by providing any piece of contentious legislation with a means of safe passage. In policy terms, the budget undermined the rationale of tariff reform (which was premised upon the inability of free trade to raise sufficient resources for both social policy and imperial defence) and therefore had to be vigorously opposed. Resisting the budget took on an even wider significance, as a symbol for defence of the existing social order and the landed class, and the point where radical Liberal initiatives should be stopped. From this miscellany of constitutional, electoral and ideological motivations, the decision of the Lords to reject the budget emerged: the deed was done in November 1909.

The decision, though perhaps justifiable in the tense political context of 1909 and in strict accordance with established constitutional powers (though unprecedented and outside the 'spirit' of the constitution), was to say the least a high-risk approach. It ignored the cardinal rule that governed the exercise of the veto between 1892 and 1895 and again between 1906 and 1909, namely that vetoed legislation should be unpopular, sectionalist and unlikely to provide an election platform for the Liberals. Of the budget, none of these things could be said with certainty. More than this, vetoing the budget set in motion a constitutional crisis that precipitated two elections, both of which Unionists lost, thereby throwing the party into chaos. It also led to the dismantling of significant portions of the constitution.

The first general election in January 1910, following quickly on the rejection of the budget, was fought on the question of the legitimacy of the Lords' action. Unionists recovered well, taking 47 per cent of the vote and 273 seats, but not enough to undermine the Liberal–Labour alliance, although the government was once again, as in 1892, left reliant upon the Irish Nationalists. The second election, in December 1910, arose from the failure of the government and the Unionist leadership to agree a compromise formula for the exercise of the Lords' veto. The result simply reinforced the verdict of January, returning 272 Unionists with 46.3 per cent of the poll. On both occasions, Unionists gained almost exactly the same number of seats as the Liberals, despite polling a larger percentage of the vote. As in 1906, it was the effectiveness of the Liberal–Labour election pact, providing greater voter efficiency and maximizing the anti-Unionist vote, that limited the number of seats gained by Unionists. At the January 1910 election, for example, where Unionists won 47 per cent of the vote and 273 seats, the same poll in 1892 had won Unionists 314 seats. In 1895 just two extra percentage points (or 49 per cent) had delivered 411 seats. Once again the Unionist vote showed an underlying stability, the polls for 1910 being comparable with those of the 1880s and 1890s. One leading historian has argued that a natural ceiling in the Unionist poll had been reached by 1910, given the unusually large turnout of voters at both elections, a conclusion that suggests that the party was locked into a cycle of permanent opposition and was in deep crisis by 1914, born of an inability to win elections (E. Green, 'The genesis of tariff reform', *Historical Journal*, 1985). On the other hand, winning 46 or 47 per cent of the vote could be interpreted as a comparatively healthy sign. It represented more support than any other party secured at the 1910 elections and was in line with polls of the late-Victorian period. Interestingly it was also respectable by twentieth-century standards, underlining the point that the Conservative position before 1914 was the product of a unique period when it confronted an effective and coherent political opposition.

However, two election defeats in a year proved calamitous for the Unionist party. Unionist faith in tariff reform as the panacea to solve all their financial and electoral problems now disintegrated. The core of Chamberlain's radical Unionist strategy had been that it could out-bid the Liberal–Labour alliance for the working-class vote, thus securing electoral dominance whilst preserving the existing social and constitutional order. But Chamberlain's policy had failed to deliver. Indeed, it was blamed by many in the party for actually costing them votes at the January election with its 'dear food' cry, a response that encouraged Balfour before December to neutralize this 'dear food' cry by tying a future tariff reform budget to a referendum. Of wider significance for Unionists, the constitution now came under sustained attack from the Liberals. The Lords' veto powers were removed in August 1911, instituting one-chamber dominance within Parliament and decisively shifting power to the executive. **[DOCUMENT XII]** With no constitutional brake upon the government, bills scheduled for 1912, including that for Welsh Church disestablishment, a bill to end plural voting (whereby property-owners had more than one vote), Irish Home Rule and a land campaign, would all become law by 1914, whether the House of Lords rejected them or not.

Removal of the two principal defensive barriers to a radical and unlimited government – the policy on tariff reform and the Lords' power of veto – sent the party into political 'free-fall'. After 1911 Unionists were in a new and very hostile political environment, without a coherent (or agreed) alternative platform with which to respond to the current economic problems and to appeal to the new electorate. Everywhere, or so it seemed to Unionists, their economic, social and political power was being systematically undercut, a realization made more acute by the spread of political militancy amongst trade unions and suffragettes. In this sense Britain was part of a wider European experience, especially in Germany, Russia and Austria-Hungary, where the Old Order and established ruling élites were rapidly losing ground in the face of modernization. An awareness of these pressures fuelled intense anxiety in the parliamentary party, culminating in the public challenge to Lansdowne's authority over the House of Lords during the Parliament Act crisis of July–August 1911, and finally forcing Balfour into retirement in November. Amongst the various social constituencies that looked to the Unionist party to defend their interests, a similar disintegrative process was at work, as witnessed by the falling membership of the Primrose League. In contrast, other leagues less closely associated with the party, the various ratepayer associations defending middle-class interests, the National Service League and the Navy League, all gained in momentum, a clear reflection of a lack of confidence in the party.

Anxiety in the party and amongst wider Conservative opinion produced a range of responses, from despair and resignation to determined resistance. The political rhetoric of Unionists at this stage is particularly interesting. It was loaded with militaristic metaphor: 'the last stand', 'to die in the last ditch' and the 'no surrender' movement of the 'die-hards'. Many came to feel, perhaps rightly, that they were in the midst of what Balfour described as 'a silent revolution', a perspective that helped to loosen traditional Conservative reverence for law and order, established parliamentary behaviour and constitutional forms, and this reached a pitch during the Home Rule crisis after 1912.

Such a feeling was particularly apparent on the right of the party, which had grown steadily since 1909. In these circles, frustration at electoral defeat and attacks upon Conservative power and influence facilitated both militancy and dynamism. With some this manifested itself in a new boldness and a willingness to think the unthinkable: a radicalism of the right (sometimes referred to as social imperialism) that sought to embrace contemporary social forces and steer them in a more socially conservative direction, in order to defend the empire, private property, the Church, Union with Ireland and the 'British' way of life. With others on the right, frustration, constant attack and intense anxiety at the future prospects of their class engendered an inflexibility and resolution (quickly sinking into atavism and reaction) that no more ground should be given up to the radical Liberal government and that cherished institutions and principles should be defended to the last.

Such sentiments on the right encouraged those who held them to mobilize against Balfour's and Lansdowne's 'flour and water' leadership (although Lansdowne survived), to organize pressure groups such as the Reveille group and the Halsbury Club, and even to moot the idea of a new party. They were also encouraged to champion extreme methods in order to resist the third Home Rule Bill after 1912. Yet the pre-war Tory right was perhaps never as strong or unified as contemporaries, and many historians, have imagined and was ultimately kept in check by an undercurrent of constitutionalism that ran through the Conservative party, if rather deeply at this stage.

Counter-revolution, 1912–1914

Balfour was replaced as Unionist leader in the Commons by Andrew Bonar Law. He faced a desperate situation, with the party out of control and directionless, divided over tactics and policy, and badly demoralized about future prospects. What was required if the party were to survive was an alternative to tariff reform: a new strategy for the party to unify around, one that would also provide a platform on which to campaign in the country to rally support back to Unionists and return them quickly to office. Guided by these considerations, Bonar Law constructed a new approach based on the defence and restoration of the constitution. This drew on party anxieties released during the political struggles since 1909, furnishing them with a focus and a mission. The approach tapped into a traditional and deeper set of conservative values and provided a common denominator that linked all the different party groupings and cliques. And in a similar fashion to Salisbury and anti-Home Rule, it could be represented as a totem around which all those alarmed by the direction in which the Liberal government seemed to be moving could unite, whatever their class, region or religion. It also disguised the fact that the party was largely barren of new ideas. It was far safer in such circumstances to campaign on older, more traditional issues. Bonar Law, in effect, was championing a Tory revival after several years of, apparently, fruitless radical Unionism.

Playing the constitutional card provided a variety of weapons with which to attack the government. These included the growth of a political spoils system as a result of the new administrative structure established to run National Insurance and the failure of the government to reconstruct a viable bicameral parliamentary system, as they had promised to do in their preamble to the Parliament Bill. Conservatives also attacked plans to disestablish the Welsh Church and to grant Irish Home Rule whilst the constitution was, in their view, suspended. It was resistance to Home Rule, however, that had the most political potential for Bonar Law's constitutional approach. According to this argument, Home Rule was illegal since no second chamber had considered it. If illegal it could (indeed, had to be) resisted until constitutionality was restored which, Bonar Law argued, would only come via an election or a referendum. This type of reasoning thrust party thinking back into the political debates of the seventeenth century, and was seen at its most dramatic in the mobilization of Ulster Unionists to defeat the imposition of Home Rule. **[DOCUMENT XIII]** It was also a dangerously open-ended rationale for it could be used to justify just about anything, such as embroiling the king in political affairs, amending the Army Annual Act or even encouraging rebellion in Ulster, before constitutionality was restored. More pragmatically, Unionist leaders believed that this type of intimidation, and especially the paramilitary build-up in Ulster, firmly backed by the Unionist party, would force Asquith to an early election on the Home Rule issue, one which they considered beneficial to them. It was a line that marshalled the Tory right behind the party leadership, albeit rather precariously, and so defused centrifugal tendencies within the party. It also invigorated the Unionist party after nearly three years of constant defeat and backsliding, in part the result of the bitterness with which Bonar Law assailed the Liberal government.

However, Bonar Law's approach never won whole-hearted support from the entire party. Tariff reform remnants struggled to keep their Chamberlainite dream alive, but they were now a spent force as shown during the chaotic resignation crisis at the end of 1912. Constructive Unionism flowed instead behind the tentative initiatives begun by the Unionist Social Reform Committee, which sought to equip Unionism with a viable raft of social policies to challenge New Liberalism. In some areas, notably over land, housing and education, the committee made progress and laid seeds that would bear fruit during the inter-war period when the Tories were back in power. However, divisions in the party, particularly with the more traditional and landed elements, and wider problems about how to finance the policies, handicapped the creation of a fully worked-out programme. Even on the issue of Home Rule, Bonar Law encountered alternative strategies, which gained in support in the party as the consequences of his own hard-line approach became more menacing. Federalism, for example, attracted much backing across the political spectrum and in Unionist leadership circles Lord Lansdowne, F. E. Smith and Austen Chamberlain were adherents in one form or another. Bonar Law never moved in that direction and even scuppered their plans, in the autumn of 1913. Down to 1914 and the outbreak of war, he remained committed to his line of forcing an election, and was sustained in this by the support of Sir Edward Carson and the Ulstermen and a vocal Tory right.

Effective stalemate was reached following the collapse of secret talks between Asquith, Bonar Law and Carson in May 1914, although the leaders tried once again in July at the Buckingham Palace Conference. Then suddenly, and to the great relief of ministers, war intervened. It removed from their shoulders an appalling set of political options with regard to Ireland. Should they partition Ireland along the lines suggested by Carson and suffer the wrath of the Nationalists? Or should they try to impose Home Rule on all Ireland even though they were unable to count on the army after the Curragh mutiny and were likely to shed the blood of Ulster Volunteers fighting under the Union Jack, and so provide a propaganda bonanza for the Unionist party? Or should they place Home Rule on the Statute Book and leave the Irish to sort out the details for themselves (a line that corresponded to Asquith's method and instinct but carried gravely unpredictable political repercussions)? It was an unenviable dilemma that appeared to work, whichever way events might have gone, against the Liberal government, and has led some historians to speculate that the Tories would have won the next election (J. Ramsden, *The Age of Balfour and Baldwin*, 86).

More recently, other historians have offered a more sceptical view of the fortunes of the Conservative party at an election in either late 1914 or early 1915. The party's actions over Ireland could well have backfired. Public opinion, if it can be gauged at all, was bored by the Home Rule crisis. In addition, Tory involvement with schemes to amend the Army Annual Act or to draw the king into political conflicts, and even to encourage army mutiny, can hardly have steered votes towards them. The Tories were in no position to take back the reins of government on the eve of war (E. Green, *The Crisis of Conservatism*). In addition, research now suggests that the Liberal–Labour pact, despite pre-war strains, would have posed a major obstacle to any possible Conservative victory (D. Tanner, *Political Change and the Labour Party*, 1990).

5. Conservative Hegemony Established, 1914–1924

Back from the brink, 1914–1918

The outbreak of war steadied the party and provided a ready escape from the full consequences of its campaign against Irish Home Rule. The Conservative leadership certainly grasped the commencement of hostilities as a much-needed sedative for a dangerously overheating party, offering Asquith, on 2 August, a party truce for the duration of the conflict, which also saw general elections suspended by an annual bill. The onset of war provided more positive benefits for the Tory party. It helped to give their various pre-war warnings of an approaching Armageddon and demands for national service, a stronger navy and economic and imperial consolidation through tariff reform, a prophetic quality that firmly identified the party with the national effort to defeat Germany. And, more generally, war re-energized sentiments and attitudes traditionally associated with Conservatives, such as patriotism, national duty and loyalty to Crown and country, as expressed in the rush to the colours by all classes. These sentiments helped to subdue (but not to erase) the explosive pressures in Edwardian society, briefly curbing trade-union militancy, suffragette protest and even Irish tensions. But perhaps most reassuring of all for the party, war diverted the government from its radical agenda, forcing Liberals into a more defensive and consolidationist outlook, something that three years of hard campaigning on the Irish issue had failed to achieve.

However, the outbreak of war and the formal party truce did not terminate inter-party rancour. Unionists' continued exclusion from office at this moment of national crisis, and their mistrust of the Liberal government's conviction in waging war, proved sources of lingering irritation. **[DOCUMENT XIV]** These tensions were initially rather muted although they surfaced at key moments, as, for example, when the entire party walked out of the Commons in response to Asquith's decision, in September 1914, to place the Home Rule Bill on the Statute Book despite a previously agreed moratorium with Bonar Law. As the conflict progressed, back-bench Tory rumblings at the government's conduct and direction steadily grew. They reflected a wider sense of unease amongst manufacturing and commercial interests, particularly once reports of shortages and administrative blunders began to filter through by the start of 1915.

These grumblings found an institutional focus with the formation of the back-bench Unionist Business Committee in January 1915, under the leadership of Walter Long. The UBC provided a valuable mechanism for political influence that did not break the party truce and so could manage Unionist dissatisfaction with the government's hesitancy in taking complete charge of the war, through military conscription or the full mobilization of industrial and labour resources. It was an early indication of a rekindling of Chamberlain-ite sympathies in the party which the wartime emergency and growing demands for greater state involvement in economic and social affairs helped to revive. By May 1915 this pool of Tory dissatisfaction was influential enough to persuade Bonar Law to enter a coalition government with Asquith. Although the pretext for this entry was the shells scandal and Admiral Fisher's resignation, its subtext was the mounting Conservative back-bench frustration at what was regarded as a lack of Liberal ruthlessness in waging the war. Unfortunately office did not assuage this anxiety, which continued to spread during 1915 and early 1916 as a consequence of Asquith's continued stalling over conscription and the junior position of the Tory leaders in the coalition.

The year 1916, however, proved to be a major turning-point in Unionist fortunes. From the start of 1916, Conservative back-bench unease was organized on a new and stronger platform, the Unionist War Committee, led by Edward Carson. The UWC enjoyed the support of over 100 Unionist MPs and proved a more effective vehicle for prodding the government, and their own leadership in the coalition, towards a more rigorous approach to the war. Its influence (and Carson's in particular) was decisive in repositioning Bonar Law alongside Lloyd George and out of Asquith's serpentine grip, especially following the Nigeria debate in November 1916 when over half the Conservative party voted against their leader. The UWC had long recognized in Lloyd George a sympathizer with their aims and proposed methods who shared a social-imperialist mentality. Once constructed, from November 1916 the Bonar Law–Lloyd George–Carson alliance was critical in establishing a new coalition government under the premiership of Lloyd George in co-operation with the Unionist party and a sizeable number of Liberal secessionists and Labour members. **[DOCUMENT XV]**

The manœuvrings surrounding the political crisis of December were confused and intricate (and are told in detail in J. Turner, *British Politics and the Great War, 1915–1918*, 1992), though it seems clear that much of the original Unionist support for Lloyd George was not intended to install him as leader but to force a thorough overhaul of government on a hesitant Asquith, even perhaps at the expense of Lloyd George himself. The plan backfired when Asquith overplayed his hand, foolishly counting on the loyalty of Unionist leaders and the seeming impossibility of them ever allying with his once radical chancellor. Asquith miscalculated his own indispensability and the office-hunger of many Unionists, a powerful tonic capable of loosening the most rigid of prejudices, even Curzon's!

The events of December 1916 were to be of immense long-term profit to the Conservative party. Expelling Asquith from the premiership split the Liberal party between a minority behind Lloyd George and the majority who followed Asquith, respectively prime minister and leader of the opposition after December 1916. The schism was not necessarily permanent and Lloyd George towards the end of the war certainly thought of a possible reunion, much as Chamberlain had contemplated in 1887 at the Round Table conference. However, what started as a temporary expedient became a more durable arrangement. The Asquithians' enmity towards Lloyd George and the bizarre logic of the parliamentary situation led increasingly to friction between the two wings and a hardening of the fracture, which was made worse by the creation of separate party whipping systems and Asquith's bitter attack on the prime minister during the Maurice debate in May 1918. The result was that the Liberal party entered the 1918 general election divided, a factor of enormous significance. For at this critical moment in the reconstruction of a modern political system, with revision of constituency boundaries and a massive extension of the franchise, the members of the Conservatives' hitherto main opposition party were at one anothers' throats.

The year 1916 also witnessed the slow eclipse of the Irish Nationalist party, the third element in the successful pre-war anti-Unionist alliance, which had bolstered Liberal governments between

1892 and 1895 and again from 1910 to 1915. This resulted from the Easter Rising in Dublin and the rapid progress throughout Ireland of Sinn Fein during the period of 1917–18, culminating in the collapse of the Irish Nationalists at the 1918 election. At a stroke, eighty committed anti-Unionist members were removed from Westminster. Simultaneously, an issue that had long poisoned British politics, and regularly activated excessive behaviour by Tories, was neutralized. Ireland would, in future, provide solid advantages for the party, furnishing a small but useful Unionist majority of seventeen Ulstermen. Once again, or so it seemed, changes in other parties delivered political dividends to the Tories.

Lastly, 1916 witnessed key developments in the organization of British industry. Under the pressures of war, industry began to consolidate, largely in response to the growing strength of trade unions. At a local level, business interests combined around District Armaments Committees. But more significantly, from 1916 industry consolidated into a national movement, the Federation of British Industry, later evolving into the National Conference of Employers' Organisations. These developments encouraged closer contacts between industry, banking and financial concerns, replacing the localist, small-scale, family-run basis of British industry with an industrial, financial and commercial sector that was now more closely integrated, better organized and with a far stronger and more co-ordinated presence in the economy and in society as a whole. This influence was increasingly put at the disposal of the Conservative party, reinforcing a trend clearly evident before 1914 and in the formation of the UBC and UWC, where industry slowly relocated itself under the Unionist banner. It gave the party vital assistance in terms of funds, expertise and an influence on the economy far in excess of anything Labour and the trade unions could wield. In turn, industry increased its own leverage in Conservative circles, transforming the party of land into the party of business.

The various advantages the party reaped from 1916 became apparent after the war and at the 1918 election. The more immediate benefit of the Conservative domination of government from 1916 was the curtailment of party strains. After a decade craving office, the coalition under Lloyd George returned the Tories from the wilderness and conferred on them ultimate control of the executive, the lack of which had been the prime source of their pre-war distemper. The new coalition added a sense of purpose to the running of the war. It overhauled the structure of government, with a War Cabinet of five giving overall direction to a host of new ministries and subcommittees. These were appointed to manage various parts of the economy, taking charge of such areas as labour, food supply, the coal mines, housing, agriculture and transport. Government extended into all parts of the economy, from the liquor trade, to chemicals and medical supplies, shifting from *laissez-faire* methods of waging war towards full-blown war collectivism. Mobilization of the state to meet the war emergency in turn generated stronger approval, among the Conservative leadership, for interventionist methods and radical Unionist solutions, rendering the low-tax, small-state inclinations which the party had inherited from Salisbury as outmoded, irrelevant and even negligent. The previously suspended constructive instincts of the tariff reformers (Bonar Law, Austen Chamberlain, F. E. Smith and Lord Milner), now the predominant leaders in the coalition, were given full license: 'Joseph Chamberlain had truly come into his own' (K. O. Morgan, *Consensus and Disunity*, 21).

It was this revival of radical Unionism that enabled Conservatives to co-operate effectively with Lloyd George. War brought out his 'Chamberlainite' qualities, which many observers and colleagues had already noticed, of boundless energy and a determination, combined with a social conscience, to defend Britain's imperial inheritance. Wartime collaboration also encouraged a centrist political ethos amongst some of the Conservative and coalition leaders which welded the Liberal progressivism of Lloyd George to a revitalized radical Unionism. An alliance of these two creeds had often been mooted before the war in the context of some form of 'national efficiency' government. The grounds for this were never propitious in the pre-war political situation that was dominated by the 'rage of party', despite the fact that both creeds were responses to the same set of problems with a clear ideological overlap between them. War and then coalition between 1916 and 1918 now provided a favourable environment for this alliance.

The general election of 1918

From late 1917 onwards, the coalition parties began to think about the end of the war. Central to their calculations was how to respond to the threat of Labour at the forthcoming general election, which was set for December 1918. War had forged Labour into a more confident and self-consciously collectivist party, with a new constitution, formulated in 1918 by Sidney Webb and Arthur Henderson, committing the party to a socialist agenda. The massive expansion in trade union membership, from four million in 1914 to seven million by 1918, meant that the party was now better financed and organized. This translated into more constituency associations, rising from 179 in 1914 to 389 in 1918, and enabling the party to break out of its electoral chrysalis and to fight for the first time as a fully independent party. The political advance of Labour was, however, accompanied by a rise in industrial militancy from 1916, with nearly six million days lost in stoppages during 1917–18, a result of the booming wartime economy. These were all developments of major consequence for Conservative leaders, particularly in light of the tense international atmosphere by 1917–18 when the war was going badly and a Bolshevik revolution occurred in Russia. British workers had ignored the Second International's call for a national strike in 1914, but several years of bloodshed in the trenches, the impact of total war at home, the creation of a socialist state in Russia and possible national defeat, might well swing them to Labour and socialism.

Matters were all the more unpredictable following the Representation of the People Act of 1918, which enfranchised all men over twenty-one (over nineteen if they were in the army) and women over thirty. This entailed a seismic shift from eight million electors to twenty-one million, with working-class voters overwhelmingly the dominant component. Nor did Conservatives have any clear indication of popular opinion, for the British electorate had not been consulted since December 1910, with annual bills after 1915 suspending elections. 'We are looking into a fog', Bonar Law declared at a special party conference late in 1917 (J. Ramsden, *The Age of Balfour and Baldwin*, 118).

Given these considerations and the absolute necessity of constructing a viable and attractive response to Labour at the election, Conservative leaders swiftly discounted the option of dissolving the coalition to fight the contest on their own. **[DOCUMENT XVI]** In the context of the immediate post-war period, most (but by no means all) considered it a dangerous line, not least because Tories had lost the last three elections. Ending the coalition would also raise the possibility of reuniting the Liberal party. Circumstances therefore recommended the continuation of the wartime coalition into peacetime, a decision dictated by political survival, and clearly reflecting the leadership's very deep sense of unease about the new peacetime world they were entering.

For the majority of Conservatives in 1918, Lloyd George represented a valuable 'pilot' to ease them into uncharted and dangerous democratic waters. He was popular as the 'little man who won the war' and would now win the peace. He also brought with him a small but useful band of Liberals who would disguise the Tory dominance behind a national label. And his pre-war radical cachet could be exploited to attract the newly enfranchised working classes away from Labour. Ultimately what mattered for Conservatives was that the existing order should be conserved. The Conservative party had always been just a means to that end (Green refers to the party as a 'guard's van'), one that might be best achieved in 1918 inside a coalition with Lloyd George rather than outside it and independent of it (E. Green, *The Crisis of Conservatism*, 125). Indeed Lord Milner, the fiercest of pre-war Tory partisans, emerged as one of the strongest supporters of a coalition with Lloyd George.

Fighting the election in harness with coalition Liberals necessitated a pre-election compact, whereby a coupon was issued to coalition candidates numbering 159 Liberals and 374 Tories. Those Tories who opposed this new direction, mostly on the party right or where constituency parties jealously guarded their Conservative representation against a couponed Liberal, felt that the party was capable of 'going it alone'. Thus, seventy-eight candidates stood as uncouponed Conservatives. However, the majority of Conservatives were persuaded of the coupon's necessity, largely by reference to the Unionist electoral alliance during the 1880s and 1890s which had resulted in twenty years of government. They were proved right. At the election of December 1918 the coalition polled a massive 53.7 per cent of the vote and gained 526 seats, composed of 335 couponed Conservatives, 133 Lloyd George Liberals, forty-eight independent Conservatives and ten National Labour candidates. Opposing them stood fifty-seven Labour members and twenty-eight Asquithian Liberals.

The scale of victory convinced the coalition Conservatives of the effectiveness of the electoral arrangement with the coupon. This was only partially true, for other factors clearly assisted them. The election had a 'khaki' flavour to it, largely because politicians had been preparing for an election in wartime when the Armistice came suddenly in October 1918. As in 1900, this rebounded to the

Conservatives' advantage as a legitimation or even perhaps a reward for those who had steered the nation to victory. The party had also gained from constituency boundary changes in the Redistribution Bill that accompanied franchise reform. Approximately thirty extra seats, mostly of a middle-class, suburban type, were created, whilst university seats and plural votes for business were preserved, all changes or continuities that worked to the advantage of the party. In addition, Tories drew on greater financial reserves with most of business now aligned behind the coalition as an effective bulwark against socialism. And party organization had recovered well from its low point in 1917 to operate efficiently on a national level.

War expanded and strengthened the middle classes, especially the lower middle classes who were drafted into wartime administration. By 1918 the number of income-tax payers (a rather crude but serviceable definition of middle class) had tripled, especially amongst the 'foreman' class, following a drop in the threshold from £150 to £130 and the general rise in wage levels during the war. The numbers holding government securities and bonds had similarly grown rapidly, a trend intensified by the investment boom immediately following the war. Ramsden has calculated that as a result of these developments over 200 'safe' middle-class, suburban seats existed by 1918, delivering a solid phalanx of Conservative-inclined voters wary of any party pledged to unorthodox financial policies, radical reform or interference with property. This constituency would increasingly find its voice by 1919–20 in the Anti-Waste campaign and demands for retrenchment.

The solidity of this middle-class Conservative vote was aided by divisions in the Liberal party. Liberal organization almost ceased to function, as local constituency associations dissolved into bickering over whom to support. This enabled Labour to establish itself as a national electoral force, winning an impressive 22 per cent of the poll with just 388 candidates. These developments were of benefit to Conservatives, enabling them to pose as the prime (indeed only) anti-socialist party. Moreover, the Liberal split shattered the pre-war Liberal-Labour electoral alliance which had held the Conservatives in check during the Edwardian period – a structural restraint that had limited the Unionist capture of seats despite achieving polls not dissimilar to those of the 1880s and 1890s. This precipitated three-cornered contests, with Labour struggling against the not inconsiderable remains of the Liberal party, particularly in their Celtic/Cornish heartlands, thereby maximizing the 'efficiency' of

Tory votes. The appearance of three-party politics and Liberal divisions were to be a major factor in the Conservative dominance of inter-war government.

The election victory of 1918 indicated some interesting trends for the Conservatives. One was the fate of the seventy-eight uncouponed Conservative candidates. Far from inviting extinction, forty-eight gained seats, suggesting that a clear, Conservative appeal could win support in the new political environment, especially an appeal that concentrated upon the threat of socialism, trade unionism and the Labour party. Many Conservatives, both couponed and uncouponed, found these fruitful lines of attack. By constructing a 'mythical class enemy, the crude (hence effective) stereotype of a unionised, militant and greedy working class', Tories were able to rally support from upper- and middle-class sections, as well as from certain working-class groups (J. Belchem, *Popular Radicalism in Nineteenth Century Britain*, 139). It also provided a clear and distinct 'other', against which Conservatives could define themselves and their creed, so creating a sense of unity and common experience. Imagining Labour as a militant, unpatriotic and sectionalist party became a staple, and most effective, electoral cry at subsequent elections. And with the Liberal party in disarray, playing the anti-socialism and anti-trade unionism card helped to lure Liberals alarmed by the growth of Labour into the Conservative camp.

More heartening was evidence that women voted disproportionately in favour of the coalition, a major consideration since women now formed between 40 and 50 per cent of the electorate and would constitute the majority after 1928. Conservatives had for many years absorbed women into the political nation through their prominent role in the Primrose League. In Conservative associations women had long held leading positions. In 1918 women's branches were established in many Conservative constituencies and a women's conference began in 1920; by the mid-1920s these innovations had attracted between two and three thousand women members per constituency. Here were the vital foot-soldiers of suburban Conservatism engaged in distributing literature, fund-raising, arranging social events, and some supporting their husbands on the platform. Women, in any case, were less inclined to vote for Labour with its trade union and strongly masculine atmosphere. In addition, M. Pugh suggests that in 1918 women were keen to show loyalty to husbands, brothers and sons who had fought and died in the war by backing the party committed to a tough peace settlement. The evidence of 1918 certainly helped to shape a number of strategies to attract the female vote, notably by refocusing upon domestic and household matters with Neville Chamberlain's reforms in the 1920s at the Ministry of Health. There were also efforts (though very hesitant ones) to remove the legal inequalities of women. The Sex Disqualification Act of 1919 opened up the professions to women and a more consensual political tone emerged in place of the rhetoric of class struggle: an emphasis on 'home and hearth' rather than 'beer and skittles', epitomized by the mild, Baldwinian Conservatism of the 1920s and 1930s.

From wartime emergency to peacetime emergency, 1918–1920

Far from easing the political situation, the onset of peace intensified problems, with a whole series of acute difficulties confronting the coalition government. Principal among these was the dramatic escalation in industrial militancy. Some thirty-four million days were lost in stoppages during 1918–19, compared to just six million in the previous year. This was made worse by the breakdown in social order in certain urban areas, such as Glasgow where in January 1919 cavalry and tanks were sent to patrol the streets. The pressing need to absorb quickly thousands of demobbed soldiers into the labour force made the situation all the more worrying. The industrial advance of Labour was also mirrored by its political progress, with a steady run of by-election victories in 1919 and 1920. In addition to these challenges to established power in Britain, many parts of the empire saw traditional authority increasingly brought into question, most dramatically in India and Ireland. And all of this was against a backdrop of revolution spreading across much of the continent with the collapse of the German, Austro-Hungarian and Russian imperial regimes.

The first priority of the coalition government in 1919 was to appease industrial labour and check the advance of the Labour party, a consideration that moved the Conservative leadership behind a thoroughgoing strategy of social amelioration. This was principally designed to preserve the newly won support of working-class voters, while defending the existing social order and retaining middle-class support. The coalition, therefore, continued the wartime boom economy in order to preserve existing high levels of employment and rising wages, operating what amounted to an 'inflationary regime' in the interests of labour, which gained job security and greater leverage for trade unions (R. McKibben, *The Ideologies of Class*, 266). Controls were also retained over many areas of the economy, especially the mines, labour, raw materials and, significantly, the rationing of food, an overtly egalitarian as well as a practical measure. High rates of income tax continued, standing at 6*s*. in the pound by 1918, compared to just 1*s*. in 1914. This sustained the high government expenditure required to fund social welfare policies, which, it was widely thought, had been placed top of the political agenda by the franchise extension of 1918. Such policies included an ambitious housing plan for 1919, increases in pensions and unemployment assistance in 1919–20, and a rise in teachers' salaries. New ministries for health and transport were also established, the latter, so many imagined, to control the railway system after nationalization. Trade boards, which set minimum wages, were extended to agricultural and engineering workers, and by 1921 some sixty-three such boards were in operation. Also in 1921, a 33.5 per cent tariff was raised on incoming goods. It appeared, then, that between 1918 and 1920 the coalition was following the rationale, certainly understandable in the menacing surroundings of 1918–19, that to become a more effective counter-revolutionary force the ministry had to become more radical. Preserving the social order required thoroughgoing, Chamberlainite remedies.

This wave of constructive government was paralleled in the imperial sphere. The Montagu–Chelmsford reforms of 1919 devolved power to local assemblies in India and, in Ireland, the coalition leaders opened secret negotiations with Sinn Fein late in 1920. Constructive government had significant political repercussions, with moves in 1919–20 to fuse the coalition partners into a National party. [DOCUMENT XVII] The idea of fusion had long been in the air. By 1919 the notion was more seriously floated as a means to 'finish the job' of reconstruction and to marginalize the growing criticism, particularly in right-wing Conservative circles, about the direction of government policy. In March 1920, Balfour formally proposed the scheme to a hesitant Bonar Law, with the vigorous support of other Conservative leaders, including F. E. Smith (now Lord Birkenhead), Chamberlain, Worthington-Evans and Milner. These initiatives drew the backing of ninety-three Conservative MPs and many more outside the party, notably from the cross-party New Members Group. They also reflected developments on the ground, where many urban constituencies were already witnessing Conservative–Liberal co-operation in a common anti-Labour alliance. As in 1918, the plan reflected Conservative unease at running again as an independent party. The idea of fusion was eventually scuppered by the coalition Liberals who were keen to retain their separate identity, much to the annoyance of Lloyd George. Although beyond the heady atmosphere of Westminster the idea was less popular among grass-roots Tories.

Back to basics, 1920–1922

By 1920 government policy began to attract serious criticism. This came from a number of directions, the most powerful being a more assertive middle class looking to defend its interests: a rebellion amongst the leafy suburbs and Victoria sponges against political tactics that sought working-class votes via policies detrimental to middle-class interests. Coalition policy had hit middle-class people hard since 1918. The financial instability caused by an overheating economy undermined the value of stocks and shares, whilst income tax at 6s. in the pound hit such people more directly. Such grievances prompted their call for a cut-back in government expenditure and a return to traditional financial orthodoxy. These demands were impressed on the party through the formation, in May 1919, of the Middle Classes Union and by agitation from local ratepayers' associations and Conservative constituency parties, particularly those affected by the coupon. These constituencies had accepted rather than welcomed the coupon in 1918, annoyed at having to stand a Conservative down in favour of a coalition Liberal but willing to abide by their leaders' advice. Constituency annoyance turned increasingly to open condemnation at the party conferences of 1920 and 1921, and pressure was put on the National Union executive to criticize the coalition. Indeed, by 1921–2 hostility towards the coalition from constituency parties was so strong that most Conservative candidates were forced to declare that they would stand as independents in a forthcoming election.

The growing demands of middle-class groups, particularly the call for reduced state expenditure, were echoed by the Treasury, the Bank of England and financial interests within the City of London, worried at the decline of Britain's financial role in the world economy. These interests enjoyed strong contacts within the

Conservative party, and from 1919–20 onwards they began to flex their muscles, demanding a return to orthodox financial and economic policies, in particular the restoration of the gold standard. Similarly, influential business interests, generally supportive of the Lloyd George coalition in its early days as the best method of combating the spread of Socialism and the Labour party, were alienated by the coalition during 1920–1 as a result of high government expenditure, high taxation and the spiralling growth of industrial militancy. Control of the trade unions had, after all, been the *raison d'être* for keeping Lloyd George.

Such 'outside' demands for retrenchment and economic orthodoxy increasingly found a sympathetic ear among uncouponed Conservatives and the Tory right, the so-called 'die-hards', of whom Lord Salisbury's Association of Unionist Peers was perhaps the most vocal and organized element. Many of their concerns were shared by a wider, if more reticent, body of Conservatives on the back benches and amongst junior Conservative ministers. Grumblings against the coalition from the Tory right were encouraged by the government's failure to deal with the House of Lords, the willingness to negotiate an Irish settlement with Sinn Fein and recent attempts at political fusion with the coalition Liberals. By 1920 their demand was that the Conservative leadership should return to more traditional, Salisburian Conservative methods: cut back the state, reduce taxation and reimpose social authority by smashing the power of the trade unions and vigorously upholding the law. **[DOCUMENT XVIII]** For these groups, the coalition was no longer a counter-revolutionary force. It was actively endangering the existing political order by creating a new one based on corporatist principles.

Those criticizing the coalition also attacked its policies on moral grounds. Much of the Conservative passion for retrenchment by 1920–1 sprang from a desire to rekindle traditional, and seemingly lost, values. High government expenditure and excessive welfare provision destroyed personal responsibility and reverence for the family. Boom conditions, by encouraging militancy and wage demands, sapped respect for established authority and the rule of traditional educated élites. An interventionist government also undermined the balance of the constitution by advancing the power and influence of trade unions, and interfered in precincts of society that were the traditional role and function of the Church, landlords and local representatives. This moral component of the retrenchment campaign was expressed in personal attacks on Lloyd

George, who lived openly with his mistress, negotiated with Sinn Fein murderers and sold peerages for money. The attack proved highly damaging to the coalition, and was utilized by Baldwin after 1922 and embellished as an integral part of his political philosophy in the 1920s and 1930s. Additionally, it is hard not to detect in this 'moral crusade' a deep vein of nostalgia: a desire to return to pre-war certainties and conventions at a time of rapid change and instability, although in fact Edwardian society had been neither very conventional nor certain.

This alliance of various groups and issues coalesced in the Anti-Waste campaign, a national protest movement launched in January 1920 under the leadership of the fourth marquis of Salisbury and enjoying press support from lords Rothermere and Northcliffe. The campaign operated at a local level, fighting by-elections by putting forward independent candidates on a platform of retrenchment and a restoration of orthodoxy. In November 1920 independents won Wrekin, then Dover in January 1921, and Hertford and Westminster in June. The Anti-Waste campaign represented a conservative revivalism in which grass-roots pressure struggled to move the party back to more traditional platforms, and so reconnecting party leaders with their primary electoral constituency – one that the late Lord Salisbury had carefully constructed during the 1880s and 1890s. In this the campaign was successful. The series of by-election successes and the obvious strength of opinion in many localities combined to shift many in the parliamentary party and the leadership away from constructive Chamberlainite solutions. The threat to their seats if they responded unfavourably to such pressure, and the strong possibility of de-selection, were more than enough to focus the mind of even the most ardent coalitionist. **[DOCUMENT XIX]**

On the other hand, it seems that the Anti-Waste campaign pushed at an open door. The altered representational basis of the parliamentary party after the war, with more professional middle-class members on the back benches and a fall in MPs drawn from landed backgrounds, made the party more sensitive to middle-class interests. This also rendered the party more homogeneous and less likely to suffer the same policy and ideological gridlock that had sapped the effectiveness of the Edwardian party. The success of the Anti-Waste campaign may be further explained by the party's awareness of the danger of a Liberal revival in the confused political environment between 1918 and 1922. In many provincial English towns and suburbs Liberals, able to capitalize on their Gladstonian legacy, posed a serious threat to Conservative seats by offering middle-class people the possibility of a strong anti-Labour protest vote, as indeed happened at the 1923 election. To meet this danger, many sitting Conservatives quickly repositioned themselves in line with their constituents and local party hierarchies, pledging to stand as independent Conservative candidates if the party entered the next election in coalition. Behind such developments lay the perception, held by many Conservatives after 1921–2, that Lloyd George was well past his sell-by date. The loss of Spen Valley and Dartford to Labour in 1919 set off a chain of defeats for the coalition that between 1919 and 1922 saw Labour capture thirteen seats, five of which were taken from coalition Conservatives. If Lloyd George could no longer hold back the onward march of Labour, then what value did he hold for the Conservative party?

This combination of pressures moved the Conservative leadership away from constructive remedies and towards retrenchment. Austen Chamberlain, the chancellor, raised the bank rate in April 1920, just two-and-a-half months after the creation of the Anti-Waste campaign, thereby initiating a 'deflationary regime' (R. McKibben, *The Ideologies of Class*, 266). This burst the economic boom, allowing unemployment to rise from 2 to 18 per cent; that in turn undercut the power of the trade unions. Manufacturing slumped to three-quarters of its 1913 level and gross domestic product to four-fifths of the 1913 level. A 'dear money' policy now set the government on course for the restoration of the gold standard, that sheet-anchor of financial orthodoxy and sound money which had been recommended back in 1918 by the Cunliffe Committee but had made little progress in the tense post-war political atmosphere. Not until 1925 was Churchill, under pressure from the Treasury, able to return to the gold standard.

The other incentive for retrenchment were the demands for cuts in government expenditure. The coalition reacted by appointing the Geddes Committee in August 1921. When its report was published, it recommended a brutal slashing of £175 million from the government's budget, particularly in the areas of housing, education and unemployment. Although not all of this £175 million was cut, Geddes 'effectively ended the era of reconstruction and foreclosed the possibility of further state expansion for some time' (J. Cronin, *The Politics of State Expansion*, 90). The coalition also restored the Treasury to its 'policing' role at the heart of British government, ensuring strict management of government finances. Thus, by 1921–2 economic policy had returned from its wartime bonanza to operate once again according to orthodox financial disciplines, fortified by its traditional institutional guardians at the heart of government.

The purpose of Tory leaders in implementing retrenchment had been to bolster party support for Lloyd George and the coalition. That support, however, failed to materialize as criticism continued to mount in Conservative circles in late 1921 and 1922. The 1921 party conference had been particularly acrimonious, with two prominent die-hards, Colonel John Gretton and Sir Henry Page Croft, attacking the premier and calling for the coalition to disband, sentiments supported by the Tory chief whip, Sir George Younger, by most southern English constituencies and by all of those in London. Back-bench opinion moved more resolutely against the coalition during 1922, alarmed by the continuing negotiations with Sinn Fein, foreign policy difficulties in Turkey and the ministry's failure to deal with the agricultural depression (the farmers' lobby was still well supported by approximately fifty Tory MPs). In addition, the anti-coalition revolt drew support from the junior ministerial stratum of government, led by Stanley Baldwin and Arthur Griffith-Boscawen, the only Cabinet ministers to attach themselves to the growing mutiny. The sympathies of the junior ministers reflected their concern about wider party unity and constituency pressure, but there was also an element of pique at the log-jam to political preferment caused by the high profile of coalition Liberals in the Cabinet. Thus, by 1922 it seemed clear that the ground had irretrievably shifted beneath the coalition, as Conservatives re-invented their party in an orthodox, financially-prudent, small-state and predominantly middle-class garb.

This revival of Salisburian Conservatism, and the growth of party animosity towards Lloyd George, raised calls to enter a future election (required by 1923 at the latest) outside the coalition. This offered the leadership two possible courses. The more extreme option was to return to full independent party operations, and aim to smash the Liberal remnants (both Lloyd Georgian and Asquithian) as a means of reinforcing the Conservative position against Labour. This was a strategy popular within many constituency parties and amongst local activists. But it found less support from those sections that could ill-afford such tactical or ideological self-indulgence, such as marginal seats in the north and Scotland or areas of local Conservative–Liberal co-operation. Thus the second and more moderate course would be to end the coalition but construct an informal alliance with coalition Liberals, under a Conservative premier, along the lines of Salisbury's co-operation with the Liberal Unionists from 1886 to 1895. This strategy appealed to the junior ministers and many in the parliamentary party, and with enough persuasion could have been sold to the wider party.

Unfortunately, the Conservative leadership opposed both approaches, demanding that the party remain wedded to the coalition. Most of the leaders continued to fear an electoral contest without Lloyd George or, even worse, one pitted against him. For Chamberlain this perception of political survival combined with a strong personal loyalty to the premier. For others, such as Balfour and Birkenhead, the return to any type of independent political stance foolishly ignored the massive economic and electoral changes since 1914. They were in any case loath to return to the stalemate of orthodox party alignments. Such attitudes exposed the wide and serious gulf that had emerged between the leadership and the rest of the party: it was the product of a misplaced conceit on the part of many leaders, who imagined themselves indispensable to the running of government, statesmen set free of grubby party tethers. This had never been a vanity of either Bonar Law or Walter Long, each of whom was forced into untimely retirement in 1921. The loss of these two overtly partisan leaders broke vital channels of communication between the front and back benches, allowing the coalition leaders to indulge themselves in displays of stratospheric immunity.

The leadership attempted to 'square-bash' the party behind the coalition by advocating a snap election, a proposal that met with a great deal of resistance. To overcome this, Chamberlain arranged a party meeting at the Carlton Club on 19 October 1922 with the intention of imposing his policy. **[DOCUMENT XX]** But he badly miscalculated both his own authority and the temper of the party, and rather foolishly rejected the moderate course of an informal alliance with the coalition Liberals, under his premiership. This forced opinion back on the less popular option of a clean break from the coalition. Critical in swinging the party behind this line was a short speech by Baldwin attacking Lloyd George for undermining party unity, and, more significantly, the intervention of Bonar Law against the coalition. Law had opportunely emerged from retirement, having left office in May 1921 a confirmed coalitionist. He was now reincarnated as the leading spokesman of orthodox, traditional Conservatism. Law offered the mutiny a 'legitimate' alternative prime minister, thus enabling the rebellion to survive the consequences of its action. When a vote was taken on the leadership's desire to continue with coalition, Chamberlain's advice was repudiated by 185 to eighty-eight votes, so effecting the most dramatic palace revolution in the party's history.

The vote split the party, slicing the leadership from the main body of the party, in a similar fashion to the split over the repeal of the Corn Laws in 1846. Chamberlain was obliged to resign as leader. It ended the coalition government at a stroke, forcing Lloyd George to tender his resignation to the king the very next day, and to enter opposition with the Conservative coalitionists. The king offered the premiership to Bonar Law, who put together the party's first independent ministry since 1905. Law's position was a weak one. He faced a formidable Commons opposition of Coalition Liberals, Asquithian Liberals, Labour and almost the entire Conservative leadership of the last decade. Coalition Conservatives refused to serve under him, sulking instead on the opposition benches where they awaited their recall once his 'second eleven' Cabinet either collapsed (through inexperience) or was tossed into extinction at the general election, which was widely thought to be imminent. The tactical consequence of the Carlton Club meeting was that the party would have to fight the election on a fully independent basis, a course forced on it by the ex-leadership, and this was something which few back-benchers relished. Going solo was something the party had not done since the 1885 election, and after four tumultuous years of government the electoral situation was uncertain and far from comforting. These worries, however, proved groundless for, at the election in November 1922 requested by Bonar Law on taking office, the party managed to repeat its 1918 success, though without the coupon, polling 38.5 per cent of the vote and reaping 344 seats.

The achievement of Conservative hegemony, 1922–1924

The 1922 election confirmed many of the trends evident in the 1918 election. Once again three-cornered contests worked to the advantage of the Conservative party by maximizing the effectiveness of its vote. This can be seen if we compare the result of the 1906 election disaster, where the Tories won 156 seats with 43.6 per cent of the vote, with the 344 seats won in 1922 on just 38.5 per cent of the vote. Similarly, disarray in the Liberal party, fighting partly as Asquithians and partly coalitionists, again benefited Conservative candidates, particularly in many southern English seats where they were able to draw into their ranks much disillusioned liberal middle-class opinion. Also, as in 1918, Labour proved a more effective propagandist target than the Liberals, vulnerable to Tory stereotypes as a militant, socialist and rather alien political force, dominated by the sectionalist interests of trade unions. Labour's clear emergence at the 1922 election, when it gained 142 seats on 30 per cent of the vote, was of long-term advantage to the Conservative party.

The year 1922 also revealed new trends. The success of the party in fighting independently eased Conservative anxieties about the new democratic world. The appeal of traditional, financially prudent, small-state Conservatism, as embodied in government policy since 1921, had proved electorally attractive, reconnecting the party to its 'natural', middle-class support after several years of flirting with Chamberlainite radical Unionism. This, in turn, was echoed by Bonar Law's election appeal in 1922, which, according to Taylor, 'sturdily promised negations' and proposed returning to a tranquil, honest, even dull, style of government, purifying the nation of the immorality (and brilliance) of the Lloyd George set, Churchill and Birkenhead (A. J. P. Taylor, *English History 1914–1945*, 254). Tranquillity was a shrewd platform for the Tories to stand on, reflecting certain popular cultural values in post-war British society that craved the recapture of a largely 'mythical' pre-war era: a world of tradition and stability, patriotism and imperial splendour, manners, morality and religious devotion. This drew sustenance from (and in turn reinforced) an emerging representation of Englishness, developing in reaction to the recent mass slaughter of the Great War and the urban, industrial stresses of the post-war world, and imagining England as a rural, calm, traditional, consensual and tolerant nation. Conservatives tapped into this miscellany of nostalgic reminiscence and images, not least because they overlapped with the increased electoral importance of English constituencies in the British political system.

Here, then, in the revival of traditional Conservative aspirations and an invocation of a tranquil, rural, English idyll were the beginnings of a new party image, one desperately needed by 1922 in order to redefine and clarify the party in the new democracy and distance it from the legacy of coalitionism. Bonar Law found this representation problematic, as a Canadian with a strong Glaswegian brogue who had made his fortune in the iron trade, and as one who was closely associated with the more frantic politics of the pre-war Home Rule struggle and with Lloyd George himself. It was left, therefore, to Stanley Baldwin (his successor as prime minister in May 1923) to weave these elements into a powerful political message that would set the tone for much of the inter-war period.

Alongside the problem of constructing a fresh image, the party also faced more immediate difficulties in 1922–3. The retirement of Law because of illness raised the likelihood of a damaging leadership struggle along the lines of 1881 and 1911. Fortunately, the matter was settled without serious divisions and Baldwin was eased into the leadership and premiership with little fuss. For insiders, the choice of Baldwin over Curzon was no real choice at all, given the former's clear advantage of sitting in the Commons, the only chamber the Labour party had representation in, and also given the fact that he had more back-bench support and the backing of Balfour. Of far more concern to party stability and performance was the ailing economy, with trade seriously depressed, agriculture hit by falling world prices and unemployment stubbornly anchoring itself at just above the million level. These economic strains exacerbated the political situation, with Labour gaining ground and confidence, and the coalition Conservatives resisting re-entry into the party fold and even, rumours suggested, looking towards co-operation with Lloyd George and (with the press support of Rothermere and Beaverbrook) a revival of coalition.

In meeting these problems, Baldwin's start was inauspicious. He decided on a positive appeal, taking up the cause of tariff reform as a means of stimulating the economy by creating employment, bolstering agricultural prices and maintaining stable demand for British commercial interests. However, tariff reform was lashed to an electoral promise made by Bonar Law, so Baldwin had to request an election in December 1923 in order to sanction it. Unfortunately, the election proved disastrous. The party's parliamentary strength fell by eighty-eight to just 254 seats, prompting criticism of Baldwin and acute party divisions over tariff policy. With tariff reform came a revival of the 'dear food' cry against the party, thereby facilitating reunion of the Liberal factions and a strong campaign by them in the country; they gained nearly fifty extra seats, mostly from Conservatives. Without a majority, Baldwin met parliament in January 1924 and forced the Liberals, alongside Labour, to vote them out of office, so precipitating the creation of the first Labour ministry under Ramsay MacDonald.

On closer inspection, the events of 1923–4 were far less desperate than they appeared. The Conservative poll had fallen by just half of one per cent on its 1922 poll, with the loss of so many seats a consequence of a temporary Liberal revival. The chances of the latter proving sustainable were remote, given the party's lack of financial resources, its inability to recruit fresh candidates, its disorganization, if not collapse, in many constituencies and the lingering animosity between Asquithians and supporters of Lloyd George. In addition, the Labour ministry was precariously reliant on Liberal votes. Clearly, it was without much of a future or much capacity to do harm.

We might argue, with hindsight, that 1923 brought positive advantages for the Tory party. Although in office for no more than nine months, this was long enough for Labour to undermine itself. Constructive policy formation, for either the long or the short term, proved impossible because of frequently bitter disagreements in Cabinet, between the party's various factions and with the trade unions. Little was done for unemployment or to solve the economic problems. Negotiations for a treaty with Bolshevik Russia, and the government's equivocation over the Campbell case, also provided invaluable propaganda for the Tories, enabling them to stigmatize Labour as extremist beneath the soft liberal words of MacDonald. By association, they also exploited the Liberal decision to bring down Baldwin's government in favour of a Labour one, and then sustain it in office, actions that reinforced the Tory claim to be the only anti-socialist force. The 1923 election had also moved the Chamberlainites back into the fold, uniting behind tariff reform which in turn polarized Liberal and Conservative politics, ending any further thoughts of a revival of coalitionism. Ironically, the policy was then speedily dropped by Baldwin, so bringing back discontented free-trade sections of the party.

Thus, when the inevitable happened and Labour collapsed in October 1924, the Conservatives were in a strong position. Instead of resigning, MacDonald requested an election, aware that Labour could make gains against a Liberal party in no position to fight a third election in just two years. It was also a highly advantageous decision for the Conservatives. With Labour and the Liberals in disarray, the election resulted in the largest ever independent Conservative victory, what one historian has called 'the forgotten landslide in British electoral history' (S. Ball, *The Conservative Party and British Politics*, 75). It set a pattern of electoral fortunes that was to last through the inter-war period. The Tories gained 412 seats on a massive poll of 46.8 per cent; although it is sobering to reflect that this was exactly the same percentage which had translated into just 272 seats in January 1910. Despite Salisbury's fears about encroaching democracy, the party seemed to perform far better on a wider franchise than on a limited one, operating in the somewhat contradictory role of seeking to tame and limit democracy whilst simultaneously its main political beneficiary. The effectiveness of the Conservative poll was built on a Liberal collapse, the party contesting just 340 constituencies in 1924 and winning merely forty seats and 17.6 per cent of the vote. Tory fortunes were clearly boosted by the Liberal withdrawal, a feature of elections during the 1930s and again during the 1950s. This had an important reverse side in that a Liberal revival would stand to retrieve lost middle-class votes and so reduce the Conservative electoral performance (as had occurred in 1923 and would again do so in 1929, 1964 and 1974). Such electoral considerations reinforced the party's chosen course after 1922, to resist Labour by destroying the Liberal party.

Victory in 1924 also helped to sharpen the party's appeal. Tariff reform was dropped, but to avoid a return to simple negativism Baldwin encouraged the reforming initiatives of many of his young ministers, amongst them Neville Chamberlain at Health, Cunliffe-Lister at the Board of Trade, Steel-Maitland at Labour and even Churchill at the Exchequer. This encouragement manifested itself in some important reforms, of the poor law, the introduction of widows' pensions and equalization of the franchise, improvements that have been labelled by historians as a 'new conservatism'. We might question how 'new' this actually was, since much of what was introduced represented ideas first formulated through the Unionist Social Reform Committee, of which most ministers had been members in the Edwardian period. And how much actual substance lies behind this useful political label? As with Disraeli's 'One Nation' slogan, 'New Conservatism' was perhaps more an exercise in marketing than a fresh start, a new rhetoric that embellished the strong traditional, low-tax, middle-class basis of Conservatism by the early 1920s with an optimistic and expansive lustre. Yet in politics image is everything, and there is little doubt that Baldwin was successful in providing the inter-war Conservative party with an attractive appeal. He drew on (and came to epitomize) the representations of Englishness, tranquillity and morality bequeathed by Bonar Law. To these he added his own personal qualities, of a self-effacing, even ordinary manner – no bad thing in a mass democracy – and a consensual approach to politics, a sensible response when the party was seeking to deny the Liberals a berth in the political system.

Since 1924 the Conservative party has dominated British government. Tory sympathizers explain the party's electoral success as an almost natural phenomenon, originating in the self-evident consonance between the British people and the Conservative party. The party, with an innate and inbred sense, has harmonized its policy and rhetoric with popular attitudes, values and concerns. However, this simplistic assessment offers little serious insight: it suffers from a Rousseauistic naïveté about how those popular attitudes reveal themselves, by whom they are interpreted (and which interpretation is right), and why it is only Conservatives who are able to read them 'correctly'. It also denies a dynamic quality to Conservative politics, rendering any clear explanation of, for example, Joe Chamberlain's tariff reform campaign or policies pursued under Mrs Thatcher problematic.

Alternatively, opponents of the Conservative party have argued that its dominance of government has been the product of deceit and corruption. The party has won and retained power only by suppressing the 'real' attitudes of the people, through various manipulative, and implicitly 'illegal', techniques, in a sort of Gramscian cultural hegemony. Control is exercised through the press and media, contacts with and the finance it receives from 'big business', the cunning management of the economy and levels of taxation, and through exploiting a parliamentary system that is slanted in its favour. But such an assessment also offers little valuable insight. Encumbered by an outmoded and simplistic Marxist reductionism, it regards the 'People' as ignorant and in possession of a pristine, inevitably socialistic, human nature. And, presumably, all the manipulative techniques used by Conservatives are available, and have been similarly exploited, by other political parties.

A stronger case could be made for explaining the Conservative party's dominance as a product of exceptionally good fortune. The best example of this would be the advantages inherited from the frequent splits and divisions within political opponents. During the period covered by this short text, the Liberals split in 1886 and again between 1916 and 1923, the Irish Nationalists were divided between 1891 and 1906, and the Labour party briefly split between 1914 and 1918. Such good fortune continued after 1924. In 1931 the Labour Cabinet fell apart, with three of the party's leaders – MacDonald, Snowden and Thomas – joining a national government, thus rendering Labour electorally impotent until 1945. During the 1950s the Labour party was again debilitated by internal divisions between a reformist Gaitskellite right wing, and a Bevanite left wing, a division that reopened with greater intensity during the 1970s. Finally, in 1981 a group of senior Labour ex-ministers split from the party, helping to form the SDP and sustain Mrs Thatcher in government throughout the 1980s.

At the same time, Conservatives have shown a remarkable ability to minimize and contain the bitter divisions which have occasionally gripped the party. This is true of the periods between 1922 and 1924 and between 1929 and 1931, the situation following the resignation of the entire Treasury team in 1958, and the events surrounding the retirement of Harold Macmillan in 1963–4. More bitter were the party strains released during the removal of Heath in 1975 and during the first four years of the first Thatcher government, 1979–83. Nevertheless, the party has ridden the storm, if with less obvious success under John Major's leadership since 1992. Such a disparity between the Conservative and Labour parties is hard to account for. Explanation may lie in the greater flexibility of Conservatism over Liberalism or Socialism, in a different background and psychology of Tory MPs, or because party members are somehow 'naturally' more fearful of splitting. In any case, to reduce the occupation of government to the persistence of good fortune is to ignore the strength of more compelling reasons.

Few of these arguments, therefore, take us far along the explanatory road. Instead, it has been argued in this text that the Conservative party's dominance of government was achieved through its ability to appeal to a wide mixture of different, and at times conflicting, communities and groups, out of which a fairly stable electoral constituency has been constructed: a constituency primarily made up of landed and commercial interests, the majority of women, the bulk of the middle classes, and a sizeable section of the working classes. This is the platform on which the party's outstanding electoral record and domination of British government since 1924 has been based.

Key developments during the period 1880 to 1924 enabled the party to construct this solid, if variable, electoral platform. One was the strengthening of certain institutions of state and society which enshrined and transmitted Conservative values. These 'Conservatizing' agencies included the growth of employers' associations, an expansion in the civil service and government bureaucracy, the development of voluntary associations, such as the Primrose League, Navy League and Territorial Army, the influence of the press, both at a provincial and national level, and an enlargement in the military services, alongside older 'surviving' Conservatizing media, such as the Church of England, the monarchy and the legal system.

A second means by which electoral dominance was achieved was the spread of party organization, both in the constituencies and at a national, co-ordinating level. Conservative organization enjoyed substantial funds, managerial expertise and local influence, which provided the party with the means to reach, influence and discipline the growing British electorate more effectively than either the Liberal or Labour parties.

Lastly, a distinctive Conservative ideology emerged during this period that linked all the various agencies, mechanisms, interests and communities, which helped to deliver to the party its electoral dominance (J. Fair and J. Hutcheson, 'British Conservatism in the twentieth century', *Albion*, 1987). It was an ideology that combined traditional values with changing contemporary beliefs and concerns. Conservatism venerated authority and hierarchy as expressed within and through the empire, the Church, the law, the monarchy, the constitution, the nation, the family and a united kingdom. In addition, it extolled interests more immediate and relevant to the new century (and in tune with its predominantly middle-class support), namely, family values of 'hearth and home', low taxation and limitations on the central state, social advancement, orthodox economic policy, free enterprise, individualism, and a desire to control working-class aspirations and politics.

Conservatism, therefore, contains an assorted mix of traditions, impulses and values. During periods of rapid change, as occurred between 1880 and 1924, a particular sequence and pattern of Conservative principles will acquire a greater appeal and clarity, in order to mediate and regulate that change within existing society (very rarely has Conservatism ever stood to resist change). Conservatism is, then, reactive to circumstances and malleable according to context, a flexibility which has enabled it to mould itself to a century of upheaval, as witnessed by its accommodation to the depression years of the 1930s, the Second World War, the unusual boom economic conditions of the 1950s and the decline of Britain's manufacturing base during the late 1970s and 1980s.

However, some political scientists have observed certain limits to the malleability of Conservative ideology and the existence of an inner pattern and rhythm. For example, W. Greenleaf has noted a tendency for Conservatism, since the late nineteenth century, to oscillate between a collectivist and an individualist approach (W. Greenleaf, *The British Political Tradition: The Ideological Heritage*, 189–346), which is similar to a division perceived by G. Searle, between a strategy of incorporation versus a strategy of containment (G. Searle, *Country before Party: Coalition and the Idea of National Government in Modern Britain, 1885–1987*, 33). According to this view party policy has tended to alternate between an expansive, interventionist, broad cross-class appeal and a more narrow, non-interventionist and limited class approach: between, in other words, a 'One Nation' and a 'Two Nations' Toryism. The balance between these competing concepts has depended, at any given moment, on political circumstances, leadership, tactics, opposition parties, intellectual movements and economic and social conditions. At key moments, the balance has tipped decisively in one direction. For example, the more narrow, limited class appeal of Salisburian Conservatism had lost ground by the early 1900s to the more expansive Chamberlainite radical Unionism, which in turn retreated with the return of a more limited middle-class Conservatism as a result of the Anti-Waste campaigns of 1919–21. Interestingly, we may identify a certain circularity here, first noticed by Jones and Bentley, that chimes with the chronology of this study: Baldwin returning the party to an outlook not dissimilar to that of Salisbury, though expressed and packaged in a very different form (M. Cowling, *Conservative Essays*, 25–40).

This dialectic continued after 1924. The onset of depression from 1929 brought another shift towards a more broad-based and interventionist strain of Toryism, ironically under Joe Chamberlain's son, Neville: a shift strengthened by military build-up and the Second World War and the arrival of the welfare state by the 1950s and 1960s. Not until the mid-1960s would the more narrow, non-interventionist and limited class appeal, most trenchantly vocalized by Enoch Powell, begin to grow strongly in party circles and for reasons similar to the earlier revival in 1919–21 – the detrimental effects on British society of high government expenditure and inflationary policies. This movement developed through the 1960s, peaking briefly between 1970 and 1972 during the Heath government, before gaining a more obvious ascendancy in the party from 1979.

Whether Conservatism is uniquely flexible, or contains an inner pattern, or is a combination of both, it has certainly benefited from economic, social and cultural changes during the twentieth century. At the core of these changes lies the rapid expansion in the size of the middle class. This was generated by the spread of property-ownership, increased suburbanization, relative economic stability, the diffusion of wealth (even, by the 1950s and 1960s, into the upper sections of the working class), the enlargement in the service sector and white-collar employment and the decline of the staple industries with the subsequent break-up of the working-class communities they sustained. Conservatism, by appealing to its interests and anxieties, has attracted the support of this large and growing middle-class constituency, in a way that the Labour party has never been able to.

Yet far from simply reflecting its aspirations, Conservatism has also helped construct the middle class, being proactive in determining its political values and goals. It has imagined a middle-class constituency into existence by carving out a working-class 'other' (propertyless, drifting, immoral, disorderly, un-respectable, uneducated, concerned solely with narrow sectional interests and its own hedonistic pleasures). Once this representation of middle-class 'self' was assembled, Conservative governments have enlarged and sustained it through public policy. The best example of this has been the legitimation and encouragement of property ownership, from the smallholdings legislation of Salisbury, to the 'cheap money' policy of Neville Chamberlain, to the property-owning democracy of Sir Anthony Eden, culminating in the privatization policies and sale of council houses under Mrs Thatcher.

However, how flexible Conservatism really is, and whether the hitherto strong appeal to much of business, the majority of women, the bulk of the middle classes and a sizeable proportion of the working classes will sustain the party in office into the next century, remains to be seen. It was the middle classes who became increasingly disenchanted in Thatcher's last years, especially over the poll tax; business interests were disillusioned by Thatcher's initially confused and later openly hostile attitude to Europe; women felt their cause had not been sufficiently advanced by the first woman prime minister; and the working classes felt they had been economically and socially discriminated against. During the subsequent leadership of John Major, the stresses and strains in the party have become only too apparent. The party is clearly going through a testing time. But whatever the outcome of the next election, if the historical record is anything to go by, Conservatism will, no doubt, successfully reshape its ideology once again.

Illustrative Documents

DOCUMENT I   Maurice Cowling on the present position

The extract is taken from a typically forthright essay by Maurice Cowling that highlights inequality, and its preservation, as a central motivation of Conservatism. Cowling was for many years a fellow at Peterhouse College, Cambridge, and an inspiration to a generation of Conservative thinkers, historians and politicians.

In the Conservative conception of freedom, in other words, there is a great deal of double-talk and many layers of concealed consciousness. Conservatives, if they talk about freedom long enough, begin to believe that that is what they want. But it is not freedom that Conservatives want; what they want is the sort of freedom that will maintain existing inequalities or restore lost ones, so far as political action can do this. And this is wanted not only by those who benefit from inequalities of wealth, rank and education but also by the enormous numbers who, while not partaking in the benefits, recognise that inequalities exist and, in some obscure sense, assume they ought to. They assume, that is to say, that a nation has to be stratified and that stratification entails privilege; and they assume this is not a matter of principle but because it is something to which they are accustomed. They are accustomed to inequalities: inequalities are things they associate with a properly functioning society and they do not need an ideological proclamation in order to accept them. They assume them pragmatically in the course of identifying themselves socially in a way they would not do if confronted with a principle.

(M. Cowling, 'The Present Position' in idem (ed.), *Conservative Essays* (London, Cassell, 1978), 9–10.)

DOCUMENT II   Edmund Burke on the nature of change

Edmund Burke's The Reflections on the Revolution in France, *published in 1790, is one of the earliest and most eloquent statements of the Conservative position. This extract from Burke considers the character of change in society, with some of its dangers and some of its benefits.*

We must all obey the great law of change. It is the most powerful law of nature, and the means perhaps of its conservation. All we can do, and that human wisdom can do, is to provide that the change shall proceed by insensible degrees. This has all the benefits which may be in change, without any of the inconveniences of mutation. Everything is provided for as it arrives. This mode will, on the one hand, prevent the unfixing of old interests at once; a thing which is apt to breed a black and sullen discontent in those who are at once dispossessed of all their influence and consideration. This gradual course, on the other side, will prevent men, long under depression, from being intoxicated with a large draft of new power, which they always abuse with a licentious insolence.

('Edmund Burke: Change and Conservation', in F. O'Gorman (ed.), *British Conservatism: Conservative Thought from Burke to Thatcher* (London, Longman, 1986), 72–3.)

DOCUMENT III   Burke on the nature of Man

Here Burke considers the complexity of human nature, believing the power of human reasoning to be inherently defective. To counterbalance this, Burke advises individuals to place greater reliance on their instincts and prejudices.

The nature of man is intricate; the objects of society are of the greatest possible complexity: and therefore no simple disposition or direction of power can be suitable either to man's nature or to the quality of his affairs. When I hear the simplicity of contrivance aimed at and boasted of in any new political constitutions, I am at a loss to decide that the artificers are grossly ignorant of their trade, or totally negligent of their duty. The simple governments are fundamentally defective, to say no worse of them . . . We are afraid to put men to live and trade each on his own private stock of reason: because we suspect that the stock in each man is small, and that the individuals would do better to avail themselves of the general bank and capital of nations and ages.

('The complexity of human nature', in R. J. White (ed.), *The Conservative Tradition* (London, Nicholas Kaye, 1957), 28–9.)

DOCUMENT IV   Quintin Hogg and the Conservative vision of society

Conservatives have long stressed the organic basis of society. Yet, as Quintin Hogg reminds us, the Conservative belief in an organic foundation to society must be placed alongside, and in harmony with, a deep conviction in individual freedom and expression.

A human community, they would say, is much more like a living being than a machine or a house. A machine or a house can be made to conform more or less to a plan. Given the materials, each can be altered more or less at will . . . If parts fall into disrepair or become outworn, they can be ruthlessly scrapped and replaced . . . By contrast living creatures are not to be so used . . . Treating their ailments is indeed a science and an art, but it is a study not the least bit like engineering. At times, no doubt, surgical operations are desirable and even necessary. But such operations are never good in themselves, and often, to save life, inflict permanent loss upon the patient.

Like creatures, human societies have individualities. These are ultimately indefinable, though they may be understood in the light of geography, economic development, scientific apparatus and racial qualities. Nevertheless, what is good for some is not necessarily good for all . . . Perfection in human societies or human individuals no more means that everyone should be alike than that perfection in horticulture would involve that all gardens should be built on one pattern, growing flowers of identical size and colour. The theory of individuality involves an understanding of individual tradition, proclivities and requirements. We do not necessarily grow more like one another as we grow better.

(Q. Hogg, *The Case for Conservatism* (London, Penguin, 1947), 27–8.)

DOCUMENT V   The Tory idea of democracy, 1885

In coming to terms with the advancing democracy, following the 1867 and 1884 Reform Acts, Tories searched eagerly for various slogans and strategies with which to win political support amongst the newly enfranchised masses. The idea of Tory Democracy was one such slogan which had been associated with Disraeli and was now taken up with gusto by Randolph Churchill. As this extract demonstrates, the term was vague, if not unintelligible, and able, as interpreted by Churchill, to support deeply traditional, Tory policies.

What is the Tory Democracy that the Whigs should deride it and hold it up to the execration of the people? It has been called a contradiction in terms; it has been described as a nonsensical appellation. I believe it to be the most simple and the most easily understood political domination ever assumed. The Tory Democracy is a democracy which has embraced the principles of the Tory party. It is a democracy which believes that an hereditary monarchy and an hereditary House of Lords are the strongest fortifications which the wisdom of man, illuminated by the experience of centuries, can possibly devise for the protection – not of Whig privilege – but of democratic freedom.

(R. Churchill at St James Hall, Manchester, 6 November 1885, quoted from R. R. James, *Lord Randolph Churchill* (London, Weidenfeld and Nicolson, 1959), 212–13.)

DOCUMENT VI   The disintegration of society, 1883

This extract is taken from Lord Salisbury's Quarterly Review *article, 'Disintegration', first published in 1883. It captures the keen sense of apprehension felt by many in Tory and aristocratic circles as a result of growing tensions within late nineteenth-century society, anxieties that Salisbury neatly wove into a wider picture of social decay and national weakness.*

The object of our party is not, and ought not to be, simply to keep things as they are. In the first place, the enterprise is impossible. In the next place, there is much in our present mode of thought and action which is highly undesirable to conserve. What we require is the administration of public affairs, whether in the executive or the legislative department, in that spirit of the old constitution which held the nation together as a whole, and levelled its united force at objects of national import, instead of splitting it into a bundle of unfriendly and distrustful fragments.

The dangers we have to fear may roughly be summed up in the single word – disintegration. It is the end to which we are being driven, alike by the defective working of our political machinery, and by the public temper of the time. It menaces us in the most subtle and in the most glaring forms – in the loss of large branches and limbs of our empire, and in the slow estrangement of the classes which make up the nation to whom that empire belongs . . . But it is in home affairs that the ominous tendency of which we have spoken is most conspicuous, and it is in these that the danger threatens us the most closely. Of course, when the word disintegration, as a possible peril of the present time, is mentioned the mind naturally reverts to Ireland: and Ireland is, no doubt, the worst symptom of the malady. But we are not free from it here; it is beginning to infect us in this country also, though the stage is less advanced and the form less acute. While scorn is thrown upon the old instincts of patriotism which animated all ranks and divisions of men with common aspirations, the temper that severs class from class is constantly gaining strength. Those who lead the poorer classes of this country are industrially impressing upon them, with more or less plainness of speech, that the function of legislation is to transfer to them something – an indefinite and unlimited something – from the pockets of their more fortunate fellow-countrymen; and it is too much to hope that a doctrine, which teaches that a disregard of the tenth commandment is the highest duty of citizenship, should not gradually impress itself upon the minds to which it is addressed. On the other hand, by a necessary consequence, the members of the classes who are in any sense or degree holders of property are becoming uneasy at the prospect which lies before them. The uneasiness is greatest among those whose property consists in land, because they have been the most attacked; but the feeling is not confined to them. No-one will say that this anxiety is without foundation. Things that have been secure for centuries are secure no longer. Not only is every existing principle and institution challenged, but it has been made evident by practical experience that most of them can be altered with great ease.

('Disintegration', in P. Smith (ed.), *Lord Salisbury on Politics: A Selection of his articles in the* Quarterly Review, *1860–1883* (London, Cambridge University Press, 1972), 341–4.)

DOCUMENT VII Salisbury's representation of the Irish, 1886

The extract is taken from a speech made by Lord Salisbury on 15 May 1886 to the National Union of Conservative Associations on the subject of the Irish question. The speech quickly gained notoriety, labelled by John Morley as 'manacles and Manitoba' and was even criticised by The Times as 'not altogether discreet'. These opinions were of little concern to Salisbury who, as a result, was able to rally the party around his more right-wing brand of Toryism.

We are to have confidence in the Irish people . . . confidence depends upon the people in whom you confide. You would not confide free representative institutions to the Hottentots, for instance . . . The habits the Irish have acquired are very bad. They have become habituated to the use of knives and slugs, which is wholly inconsistent with the placing of confidence in them . . . (a portion of them) murder agents, they mutilate cattle, they prevent harvest men earning their livelihoods, they shoot people in the legs who presume to pay their lawful debts and by these actions and threats . . . they punish all who give any support or have any dealings with the supporters of the existing polity . . . My alternative policy is that Parliament should enable the government of England to govern Ireland. Apply that recipe honestly, consistently and resolutely for twenty years and at the end of that time you will find that Ireland will be fit to accept any gifts in the way of local government . . . what she wants is government – government that does not flinch, that does not vary – a government she cannot hope to beat down by agitations at Westminster.

(The Times, 17 May 1886.)

DOCUMENT VIII Chamberlain and Radical Unionism, 1891

As Salisbury's second ministry ran out of steam, Joseph Chamberlain sought to re-enthuse the Unionist alliance and its popular support with a more constructive appeal, in a speech at Portsmouth in April 1891. His agitation for a more progressive policy had little impact on the Unionist leadership at this stage. None the less, the speech illuminates a line of continuity in Chamberlain's career, namely his pursuit of a more radical, interventionist political course, a line that would prove more successful in converting the party after 1903.

Small-holdings and allotments for the labourer, free education for all – those are important points in any social programme; but they do not exhaust it. The amendment of the factory acts, extension of public health acts, further provisions for securing sanitary dwellings for the working classes – these are all included . . . all these things that deal with the material condition of the people are within your grasp and they must be realised within the next few years, where as they cannot be even approached by the Gladstonians so long as Home Rule is tied like a mill-stone round their necks (cheers), and prevents them from taking any steps in the direction of domestic reform. Now the proposals which I have made to you would promote the education of your children. They would do something, as I think, to better your average condition, and above all, to raise the status of what is now the lowest class of the labouring population: but when all has been done that can be done in this direction, there are still cases of accident, causes of sickness and the case of old age and of incapacity to work would require to be provided for.

(The Times, 3 April 1891.)

DOCUMENT IX   Churchill and Radical Toryism, 1886

In November 1886 Randolph Churchill, Salisbury's chancellor, began to agitate for a more radical brand of Toryism. This letter, written by Lord Salisbury to Churchill on 7 November, was a measured warning against such a course, and came just a month before Churchill resigned in December 1886. The letter reflects Salisbury's 'quietist' approach to party affairs and neatly encapsulates the basic dialectic of Conservative political tactics over the next forty years.

The Tory party is composed of varying elements . . . the classes and the dependents of class are the strongest ingredients in our composition, but we have so to conduct our legislation that we shall give some satisfaction to both classes and masses. This is specially difficult with the classes – because all legislation is rather unwelcome to them, as tending to disturb a state of things with which they are satisfied. It is evident, therefore, that we must work at less speed and at a lower temperature than our opponents. Our bills must be tentative and cautious, not sweeping and dramatic . . . The opposite course is to produce drastic, symmetrical measures, hitting the classes hard, and consequently dispensing with their support, but trusting to public meetings and the democratic forces generally to carry you through. I think such a policy will fail. I do not mean that the classes will join issue with you on one of the measures which hits them hard, and beat you on that. That is not the way they fight. They will select some matter on which they can appeal to prejudice, and on which they think the masses will be indifferent; and on that they will upset you.

(Salisbury to Churchill, 7 November 1886, in B. Coleman, *Conservatism and the Conservative Party in Nineteenth Century Britain* (London, Edward Arnold, 1988), 177.)

DOCUMENT X   Chamberlain and tariff reform, 1903

In September 1903 Joseph Chamberlain resigned from the government in order to campaign in the country on behalf of his new policy of tariff reform, unrestrained by Cabinet collective responsibility. Both extracts are taken from his speech delivered at St Andrews Hall, Glasgow, on 6 October 1903.

What are our objects? They are two. In the first place, we all desire the maintenance and increase of the national strength and the prosperity of the United Kingdom . . . Britain has played a great part in the past in the history of the world, and for that reason I wish Britain to continue. Then, in the second place, our object is, or should be, the realisation of the greatest ideal which has ever inspired statesmen in any country or any age – the creation of an empire such as the world has never seen. We have to cement the union of the states beyond the seas: we have to consolidate the British race: we have to meet the clash of competition . . . we have to meet it no longer as an isolated country; we have to meet it fortified and strengthened, and buttressed by all those of our kinsmen, all those powerful and continually rising states which speak our common tongue and glory in our common flag.

*   *   *

Our imperial trade is absolutely essential to our prosperity at the present time. If that trade declines, or if it does not increase in proportion to our population and to the loss of trade with foreign countries, then we will sink at once into a fifth-rate nation. Our fate will be the fate of the empires and kingdoms of the past . . . I have said if our imperial trade declines we decline . . . It will decline inevitably unless while there is still time we take the necessary steps to preserve it. Have you ever considered why it is that Canada takes so much more of the products of British manufacturers than the United States of America does per head? Why does Australia take about three times as much per head as Canada? Why does South Africa . . . take more per head than Australasia? When you have got to the bottom of that – and it is not difficult – you will see the whole argument. These countries are all protective countries.

('The Case for Tariff Reform', in C. W. Boyd (ed.), *Mr Chamberlain's Speeches* (London, Constable, 1914), vol.2, 140–64.)

DOCUMENT XI   The threat of Labour, 1905

At the general election of 1905 the Conservative party slumped to its lowest parliamentary total of 156 seats. Here Arthur Balfour, writing to his aunt, Lady Salisbury, reflects on the implications of the defeat and in particular the wider significance of the Labour party's trawl of some thirty seats.

I am horribly ashamed at feeling a kind of illegitimate exhilaration at the catastrophe that has occurred. It has made me more violently and pleasurably interested in politics than I remember having been since the Home Rule bill. If I read the signs aright, what has occurred has nothing whatever to do with any of the things we have been squabbling over the last few years. C.B. [Campbell-Bannerman] is a mere cork, dancing on a torrent which he cannot control, and what is going on here is the faint echo of the same movement which has produced massacres in St Petersburg, riots in Vienna and Socialist processions in Berlin. We always catch continental diseases, though we usually take them mildly.

(Arthur Balfour to Lady Salisbury, January 1906, in B. E. C. Dugdale, *Arthur James Balfour: First Earl of Balfour* (London, Hutchinson, 1939), vol.1, 329.)

DOCUMENT XII   Loss of the Lords' veto, 1910

*Having lost two general elections in 1910 and informed by the prime
minister in July of a pledge from the king to exercise his royal prerogative
to create more peers, if the government's Parliament Bill was defeated in
the House of Lords, Lansdowne and Balfour recommended abstention to
the Unionist peers in order to allow the bill through with the support of the
Liberal peers. The policy of 'surrender' raised violent opposition in the
party, led by Lord Halsbury and a number of peers who were determined
to ignore their leaders' advice, defeat the bill and 'damn the consequences'.
The rebels' (ditchers') plans were thwarted by a splinter group of Unionist
peers, led by Lords Curzon and Midleton, who voted for the bill.*

A disastrous week, as I think, in English history. We began on
Monday with a vote of censure by Balfour on the Govt. for
unconstitutional dealing with the royal prerogative. This move was
welcomed as a sign of reviving vigour in Balfour & he made a good
speech, but the thing fell flat for a want of more vehement language.
On Tuesday, however, when we had the debate on the Lords'
amendments, the honours were clearly on our side, owing to three
fine fighting speeches by Hugh Cecil, Carson and Bonar Law. On
Wednesday we had the belated second reading of the finance bill. On
Thursday the H. of Commons passed the resolution to provide £400
a year payment for each member other than Govt. officials, whilst
the House of Lords ended an honourable and distinguished career of
700 years or so by a miserable capitulation on the Parliament bill,
rather than face the consequences of the radical threat to create an
unlimited number of Peers. The event was all the more degrading by
the fact that 13 Bishops, and from 30 to 40 Unionist Peers voted
with the Govt. & turned what would have been a certain defeat into
a radical victory by a majority of 17. I cannot speak or write the
disgust I feel at this despicable surrender, just when I hoped that
accidentally the consequences of bad and dilatory leadership were
possibly going to be avoided by the action of Ld. Halsbury and his
stalwart colleagues. I write 'de profundis' & will say no more.

(Bridgeman Diary, 6–12 August 1911, in P. Williamson (ed.), *The
Modernisation of Conservative Politics: The Diaries and Letters of William
Bridgeman, 1904–1935* (London, Historians Press, 1988), 48–9.)

DOCUMENT XIII Bonar Law on Ulster, 1912

At Blenheim Palace on 29 July 1912, the recently appointed Conservative leader, Andrew Bonar Law, delivered one of the most remarkable and inflammatory speeches by any British political leader. In the course of attacking the third Home Rule bill which the government had introduced just four months previously, he committed the Conservative party to support civil war in Ireland if the Liberal ministry did not gain the sanction of the people beforehand. It set the tone for what proved to be a very acrimonious political struggle.

In our opposition to them (the Govt) we shall not be guided by the considerations or bound by the restraints which would influence us in an ordinary constitutional struggle. We shall take the means, whatever means seem to us most effective, to deprive them of the despotic power which they have usurped and compel them to appeal to the people whom they have deceived. They may . . . carry their Home Rule bill through the House of Commons but what then? I said the other day in the House of Commons and I repeat here that there are things stronger than Parliamentary majorities . . . In my belief, if an attempt were made to deprive these men (Ulstermen) of their birthright – as part of a corrupt Parliamentary bargain – they would be justified in resisting such an attempt by all means in their power, including force. I said it then and I repeat now with a full sense of the responsibility which attaches to my position, that, in my opinion, if such an attempt is made, I can imagine no length of resistance to which Ulster can go in which I should not be prepared to support them, and in which, in my belief, they would not be supported by the overwhelming majority of the British people.

(R. Blake, *The Unknown Prime Minister: The Life and Times of Andrew Bonar Law* (London, Eyre & Spottiswoode, 1955), 130.)

DOCUMENT XIV The party truce and Tory frustrations, 1915

The intense bitterness between the parties during the period 1911–14 did not disappear with the outbreak of war. Tensions continued below the surface, despite the party truce. By the spring of 1915 they were strong enough to see the formation of the Unionist Business Committee under

*Walter Long's chairmanship which compelled Bonar Law, on 17 May, to
enter a coalition with Asquith.*

May 1915.   All the time we have been going on abstaining from
forcible criticism, when we might have been doing good by calling
public attention to reveal points in which the action of the Govt. has
done harm, and will do more, if they do not mend their ways. Such
matters as

(1) The suppression of unfavourable news, and the secrecy as to
the progress of recruiting etc. The nation does not want to be treated
as a child, and will never wake up until the real situation is revealed,
and until every man realises the gravity of the danger, and the fact
that it requires a gigantic effort to end the war. The nation is sound
and will respond to any clear call but it must be clear.

(2) The interference of politicians in naval and military matters
such as Winston's Antwerp expedition and the more recent
Dardenelles adventure.

(3) The utter incompetence of those who are supposed to be
dealing with aliens.

But our leaders seem to have allowed themselves to accept the
position that the 'truce' involves abstention from all serious and
sustained criticism, where as it really never meant anything more
than abstention from discussion of party controversies and questions
in dispute with the war.

(Bridgeman Diary, in P. Williamson (ed.), *The Modernisation of Conservative
Politics*, 83–4.)

DOCUMENT XV   Formation of the Lloyd George coalition, 1916

*As tensions ran increasingly high both between and within the parties and
with the war going badly, an acute political crisis developed early in
December 1916. It resulted in the removal of Asquith as prime minister
and his replacement by Lloyd George at the head of a predominantly
Conservative coalition.*

The history of the crisis is so well known that I need not expatiate upon
it. But there are one or two points that may have escaped attention.

It is true L.G. was very unpopular with his own side & with Labour, but one thing Asquith & Co had not calculated was the strength of a new premier who has a lot of appointments at his disposal, & many more Liberals remained with L.G. than was expected, simply in the hope of getting something. Labour was also won over by the opportunity of office quite out of proportion to their numbers.

Another curious point is the way B. Law was induced to throw Asquith over; but in my opinion his desire for a reconciliation with Carson, whose Nigerian debate he felt most bitterly, was a very powerful influence. I think he leans very much on a strong man like Carson & feels himself unequal to his task alone. I do not believe there was a Unionist cabinet minister who would not have preferred Asquith to L.G. as a leader. But they were all afraid of an election & also genuinely anxious to have a small war cabinet and more vigour.

The Asquithian excuse for their downfall which attributed it all to a press plot will not hold water. The power of the press is greatly exaggerated, but apart from that L.G. needed no plot. All he had to do was hold a pistol at Asquith's head whenever he chose, because he was the strongest man. He has carried the Liberal party on his back for eight years, & however unpopular or mistrusted he was in the house, he carried much more weight in the country than Asquith, who was almost everywhere looked on as a lazy & dilatory man.

(Bridgeman Diary, autumn 1917, in P. Williamson (ed.), *The Modernisation of Conservative Politics*, 111–12.)

DOCUMENT XVI   Wartime coalition into peacetime coalition, 1918

With the sudden and somewhat unexpected collapse of Germany late in 1918, the necessity for a general election grew ever more pressing; it was eight years since the people were last canvassed. Realizing the post-war period would be difficult, and with no prospect or desire of returning to the Liberal fold, Lloyd George was keen to continue the coalition in peacetime. Bonar Law and many Conservative leaders, similarly worried by the problems of peace, shared Lloyd George's desire for continuation, recognizing the prime minister to be a valuable political asset in an uncertain world.

My Dear Bonar Law,

The more I think of it the more convinced I become that there ought to be a general election, and that the sooner it can be arranged, subject to the exigencies of the military position, the better. We have discussed this so often that I need not go at length into my reasons for this view. My principal reason is that I believe it is essential that there should be a fresh parliament, possessed of the authority which a general election alone can give it, to deal with the difficult transition period which will follow the cessation of hostilities.

If there is to be an election I think it would be right that it should be a coalition election, that is to say, that the country should be definitely invited to return candidates who undertake to support the present government not only to prosecute the war to its final end and negotiate the peace, but to deal with the problems of reconstruction which immediately arise directly an armistice is signed . . . I should myself desire to see this arrangement carried through on personal grounds, for during the last two years I recognise that I have received the whole-hearted support of your party, and that the government has had a unity both in aims and in action which has been very remarkable in a coalition government. I am convinced also that such an arrangement will be the best for the country. The problems with which we will be faced immediately on the cessation of hostilities will be hardly less pressing and will require hardly less drastic action than those of the war itself. They cannot, in my opinion, be dealt with without disaster on party lines. It is vital that the national unity which has made possible victory in war should be maintained until at least the main foundations of national and international reconstruction have been securely laid.

(Lloyd George to Bonar Law, 2 November 1918, in J. Ramsden (ed.), *Real Old Tory Politics: The Political Diaries of Sir Robert Sanders, Lord Bayford, 1910–1935* (London, Historians Press, 1984), 144–5.)

DOCUMENT XVII   Attempts to fuse the Conservative party and the Lloyd George Liberals, 1920

Against a background of growing unpopularity of the coalition government, moves began early in 1920 to fuse Conservatives and coalition Liberals into a grand centrist or national party. Many Tory leaders supported the idea, including Balfour to whom this letter, from a more sceptical Bonar Law, was addressed.

L.G. first of all met his Liberal ministers and he found that they were much more frightened at the idea of losing their identity as Liberals than he had expected. In consequence when he met the coalition Liberals as a whole he spoke only of the need for closer co-operation . . . The result of this will probably be not to attempt any real fusion of the parties but to get co-operation, something on the lines of the Liberal Unionists and Conservatives in the early days. This will be very difficult to arrange and will certainly not be efficient but personally I am not sorry at the turn events have taken. I do not like the idea of complete fusion if it can be avoided, but I had come to think, as you had also, that it was really inevitable if the coalition were to continue. But it always seemed to me more important from L.G's point of view than from ours. As a party we were losing nothing and, since the necessity of going slowly in the matter has come from L.G.'s friends, I do not regret it.

(Bonar Law to Balfour, 24 March 1920, in R. Blake, *The Unknown Prime Minister*, 416–7.)

DOCUMENT XVIII   The rise of anti-coalition sentiment, 1919

The extract is an early indication of growing unease at the coalition's economic policy. It takes the form of an election address delivered by the prospective Conservative candidate for the Isle of Thanet by-election in November 1919, Esmond Harmsworth. The candidate was the twenty-one-year-old son of Lord Rothermere, the newspaper owner who within just a few months would co-launch the Anti-Waste League, enshrining many of the points in the address.

Waste is still going on in every direction and in addition the country is threatened with an education act, the cost of which no one has been able to estimate: with a housing act that will cost not less than £300,000,000 and with an enormous expenditure in many other directions. The government seems quite incapable of stopping this wasteful and extravagant expenditure. Instead the country is threatened with a great increase in income tax and since the profiteering act came into force the cost of living has gone up from 120% to 128%, above war prices. These greatly increasing demands press with crushing effect upon every individual and every household. Unless they are stopped they will lead to irretrievable disaster. I stand as a candidate first and foremost as an unrelenting opponent of this extravagance and as a determined advocate of the policy that national expenditure must be cut down to at least the level of national income.

(The Times, 1 November 1919.)

DOCUMENT XIX   The Anti-Waste campaign, 1921

The Anti-Waste League, active since 1919, had struggled to convert sitting candidates to their cause under the threat of standing an Anti-Waste opponent at by-elections. The extract is taken from The Times *editorial of 9 June 1921, during the by-election at St George's, Westminster, where the Anti-Waste candidate, James Erskine, defeated the Conservative, Sir Herbert Jessel. It highlights the disenchantment felt by many in the coalition government.*

How wasteful and how unprincipled this government has been the country is only now beginning to clearly perceive. It has maintained itself on false pretences, it has eroded and undermined the constitutional control of the House of Commons, it has disorganised the cabinet itself, it has jeopardised our foreign relations in a dozen directions, it has suffered our trade and industry to fall through chaos into paralysis and it has reached a position in which its word is trusted by no sincere man . . . There are only three remedies – strict economy, hard work and sound policy . . . The war habit of relying upon the government for guidance and leadership must be discarded and the people of this country must begin to help themselves. The election at St George's, Westminster, points the way, though it will not be enough to merely elect Anti-Waste candidates. The first need of the country is, indeed, retrenchment and the parsimonious administration of public finance. In order that this may be fully met during the difficult years that lie before us, it is necessary that we should be governed by transparently honest and single-minded men who will command public confidence because they seek . . . to serve the community and to uphold its constitutional liberties.

(*The Times*, 9 June 1921.)

DOCUMENT XX   The Carlton Club rebellion, 1922

The extract taken from the Bridgeman diary recounts events at the Carlton Club meeting on 19 October 1922 when, by 185 votes to eighty-six, the Conservative party elected to leave the coalition. Austen Chamberlain resigned the party leadership and led most of his fellow coalitionists into opposition against the first purely Conservative ministry since 1905, led by Bonar Law.

At the meeting everyone was very restrained and very sad at having to ventilate our differences with our leader, who made a long and most unconvincing speech about the necessity of preserving the coalition – which was not assisted by the news just received that the independent Conservative had won the Newport election. Then Baldwin made a short speech the other way – very much to the point – calling attention to the disintegrating effect Lloyd George had on his own party and was beginning to have on ours. E. Pretyman and G. Fox moved and seconded their motion in brief and well chosen words and F. Mildmay supported it and Sir H. Craik made a vehement attack on Indian, Irish and Egyptian policies, which no one listened to, and then Bonar rose and at first kept us doubtful as to his views, but later came down unreservedly on our side. His speech made a great deal of difference to the result. If he had not come I think we should have won. If he had spoken for the coalition I am pretty sure we should not. Austen took it very well and most of the 86 who voted with him were really rather glad to be beaten, except a few Scots who think they will lose their seats. Whichever way the vote had gone I should have had to resign. As it was I resigned because I had to vote against my leader. The other way I should have resigned because I would not go to the election as a member of the coalition Govt. Now Bonar Law is trying to form a government and no doubt will succeed and probably dissolve in 2 or 3 days, so that the new house can meet and pass the Irish Constitution bill . . . L.G. has begun touring the country with very egotistic speeches and ill-concealed annoyance and abuse of the

Carlton Club and die-hards and not a word of thanks to the party that has kept him in office so long. I wonder what the effect will be, but I can't think it will be very good for him. The people who voted for Austen will go to the election as Unionists, I think, submitting to the decision of the party, except perhaps F.E. [Lord Birkenhead] who might join L.G. The more aspiring of my colleagues are on Bonar's doorstep, looking for high office or getting the press to publish their photograph and say how indispensable they are. I hope I may get some slight promotion after Steel-Maitland, Lloyd-Greame and Joynson Hicks are satisfied, but may perhaps only be asked to go on where I am. If the latter I shall regard myself as having got as high as I am likely to get and possibly retire from politics before very long. L.G. seems in a very excited mad mullahish state and regards himself I think as the messiah – though I am sure the last thing he wishes is to be crucified for anyone else, rather the contrary . . . One thing is certain about the crisis is that it certainly was not the result of a Carlton Club plot, but came up from below with great force from the constituencies.

(Bridgeman Diary, October 1922, in P. Williamson (ed.), *The Modernisation of Conservative Politics*, 161–2.)

Bibliography

General texts

Good introductions include R. Blake, *The Conservative Party from Peel to Thatcher* (London, Fontana, 1985); D. Southgate, *The Conservative Leadership, 1832–1932* (London, Macmillan, 1974); and Lord Butler (ed.), *The Conservatives: A History from their Origins to 1965* (London, Allen & Unwin, 1977). Pride of place goes to the Longman series on the history of the Conservative party, which now comprises R. Stewart, *The Foundation of the Conservative Party* (London, Longman, 1978); R. Shannon, *The Age of Disraeli, 1868–1881* (London, Longman, 1992) and *The Age of Salisbury, 1881–1902* (London, Longman, 1996); and J. Ramsden, *The Age of Balfour and Baldwin, 1902–1940* (London, Longman, 1978). More recent general studies include A. J. Davies, *We, The Nation: The Conservative Party and the Pursuit of Power* (London, Little Brown and Company, 1995) and a recent collection of essays, M. Francis and I. Zweiniger-Bargielowska (eds.), *The Conservatives and British Society, 1880–1990* (Cardiff, University of Wales Press, 1996).

Few other studies span the nineteenth and twentieth centuries, most tending to start or break in 1900, 1914 or 1918. This caveat aside, a great deal can be gleaned from B. Coleman's excellent *Conservatism and the Conservative Party in Nineteenth Century Britain* (London, Edward Arnold, 1988); S. Ball's lucid and valuable *The Conservative Party and British Politics, 1902–1951* (London, Longman, 1995); P. Norton and A. Aughey, *Conservatives and Conservatism* (London, Temple Smith, 1981); A. Gamble, *The Conservative Nation* (London, Routledge & Kegan Paul, 1974); T. Lindsay and M. Harrington, *The Conservative Party, 1918–1970* (London, Macmillan, 1979); and, more comprehensively and thematically, A. Seldon and S. Ball (eds.), *Conservative Century: The Conservative Party since 1900* (Oxford, Oxford University Press, 1994).

Conservative party organization and ideas

Party organization can be approached through R. McKenzie, *British Political Parties: The Distribution of Power within the Conservative and Labour Parties* (London, Heinemann, 1963); S. Beer, *Modern British Politics: A Study of Parties and Pressure Groups* (London, Faber, 1965); E. J. Feuchtwanger, *Disraeli, Democracy and the Tory Party* (Oxford, Oxford University Press, 1968); chs.4–7 of Norton and Aughey, *Conservatives and Conservatism;* M. Pugh, *The Tories and the People, 1880–1935* (Oxford, Blackwell, 1985); chs.2–7 of Seldon and Ball, *Conservative Century . . .* ; J. P. Cornford, 'The transformation of Conservatism in the late nineteenth century', *Victorian Studies,* 7 (1963–4), 35–66, and 'The parliamentary foundations of the Hotel Cecil', in R. Robson (ed.), *Ideas and Institutions of Victorian Britain* (London, Bell, 1967); M. Pugh, 'Popular Conservatism in Britain: continuity and change 1880–1987', *Journal of British Studies,* 27 (1988), 254–82; S. Ball, 'The 1922 Committee: the formative years, 1922–45', *Parliamentary History,* 9 (1990), 129–57; and 'Parliament and politics in Britain 1900–1951', *Parliamentary History,* 10 (1991), 243–76.

Despite its age, Edmund Burke's *Reflections on the Revolution in France* (edited by W. Todd) (New York, Rhinehart, 1959), remains a seminal text for understanding Conservative 'positions', as are P. Smith (ed.), *Lord Salisbury on Politics* (Cambridge, Cambridge University Press, 1972); H. Cecil, *Conservatism* (London, Willams & Norgate, 1912); Q. Hogg, *The Case for Conservatism* (London, Penguin, 1947); R. Scruton, *The Meaning of Conservatism* (London, Macmillan, 1980); and M. Cowling (ed.), *Conservative Essays* (London, Cassell, 1979). Conservative thinkers and thinking can also be investigated through a variety of anthologies: R. J. White, *The Conservative Tradition* (London, Nicholas Kaye, 1950); I. Gilmour, *Inside Right: Conservatism, Policies and the People* (London, Hutchinson, 1977); F. O'Gorman, *British Conservatism: Conservative Thought from Burke to Thatcher* (London, Longman, 1986); R. Eccleshall, *English Conservatism since the Restoration* (London, Unwin & Hyman, 1990). Analyses of Conservatism and Conservative beliefs have grown quickly in the last two decades. The most notable studies are N. O'Sullivan, *Conservatism* (London, Dent, 1976); W. Greenleaf, *The British Political Tradition: The Ideological Inheritance* (London, Methuen, 1983); R. Nisbet, *Conservatism: Dream and Reality* (Milton Keynes, Open University

Press, 1986); R. Eatwell and N. O'Sullivan, *The Nature of the Right: American and European Politics and Political Thought since 1789* (London, Pinter, 1989); T. Honderich, *Conservatism* (London, Penguin, 1990); A. Aughey et al., *The Conservative Political Tradition in Britain and the United States* (London, Pinter, 1992); H. Glickman, 'The Toryness of British Conservatism', *Journal of British Studies*, 25 (1961), 111–43; J. D. Fair and J. A. Hutcheson, 'British Conservatism in the twentieth century: an emerging ideological tradition', *Albion*, 19 (1987), 549–578; and an excellent chapter by J. Barnes, 'Ideology and factions', in Seldon and Ball, *Conservative Century* (1994).

Salisbury and the Conservative ascendancy, 1885–1900

Good entrées to this period are B. Coleman, *Conservatism and the Conservative Party*, ch.6; M. Pugh, *The Making of Modern British Politics, 1867–1939* (London, Blackwell, 1982), ch.3; and E. J. Feuchtwanger, *Democracy and Empire* (London, Edward Arnold, 1985), ch.6. Of the more detailed studies, three are essential reading: P. Marsh, *The Discipline of Popular Government: Lord Salisbury's Domestic Statecraft, 1881–1902* (London, Harvester, 1978); A. Offer, *Property and Politics, 1870–1914: Landownership, Law, Ideology and Urban Development in England* (Cambridge, Cambridge University Press, 1981); and E. H. H. Green, *The Crisis of Conservatism: The Politics, Economics and Ideology of the British Conservative Party, 1880–1914* (London, Routledge, 1995). See also M. Pinto-Duschinsky, *The Political Thought of Lord Salisbury, 1854–68* (London, Constable, 1967); R. McKenzie and A. Silver, *Angels in Marble: Working Class Conservatives in Urban England* (London, Heinemann, 1968); H. Pelling, *The Social Geography of British Elections, 1885–1910* (London, Macmillan, 1967); K. D. Brown, *Essays in Anti-Labour History: Responses to the Rise of Labour in Britain* (London, Macmillan, 1974); K. Young, *Local Politics and the Rise of Party: The London Municipal Society and the Conservative Intervention in Local Elections* (Leicester, Leicester University Press, 1975); M. Pugh, *The Tories and the People* (Oxford, Blackwell, 1985); Lord Blake and H. Cecil (eds.), *Salisbury: The Man and his Policies* (London, Macmillan, 1987); M. Fforde, *Conservatism and Collectivism, 1886–1914* (Edinburgh, Edinburgh University Press, 1990); and J. E. Cronin, *The Politics of State Expansion: War, State and*

Society in Twentieth Century Britain (London, Routledge, 1991), chs.1–4.

Ireland played a key role in Conservative affairs during the late nineteenth century and its importance can be examined in A. Cooke and J. Vincent, *The Governing Passion: Cabinet Government and Party Politics in Britain, 1885–1886* (London, Harvester, 1973); A. Gailey, *Ireland and the Death of Ireland: The Experience of Constructive Unionism, 1890–1905* (Cork, Cork University Press, 1987); and A. Jackson, *The Ulster Party: Irish Unionists in the House of Commons, 1884–1911* (Oxford, Oxford University Press, 1988). Whilst this present study generally steers clear of imperial and foreign policies, their domestic and party implications can be gleaned from B. Porter, *Britain, Europe and the World, 1850–1986* (London, Longman, 1983); A. Friedberg, *The Weary Titan: Britain and the Experience of Relative Decline, 1895–1905* (Princeton, Princeton University Press, 1988); P. Cain and A. Hopkins, *British Imperialism: Innovation and Expansion, 1688–1914* (London, Longman, 1993); and A. Porter, 'Lord Salisbury, foreign policy and domestic finance, 1860–1900', in Blake and Cecil (eds.), *Salisbury: The Man and his Policies* (1987). Most of the key players have had biographies written about them, of which the best are: R. Foster, *Lord Randolph Churchill: A Political Life* (Oxford, Oxford University Press, 1981); and R. Jay, *Joseph Chamberlain: A Political Study* (Oxford, Oxford University Press, 1981). For Salisbury, the biographies by R. Taylor and A. L. Kennedy are poor, so G. Cecil, *The Life of Robert, Marquis of Salisbury* (1921–31), remains the best, whilst useful insights are in R. Harcourt-Williams (ed.), *The Salisbury–Balfour Correspondence, 1869–1892* (Hertford, Hertfordshire Record Office, 1988). Fresh studies of Salisbury are needed, in addition to Shannon's, with A. Roberts's authorized biography forthcoming.

Several articles warrant particular mention, in addition to those by M. Pugh and J. Cornford already cited: H. Cunningham, 'The Conservative party and patriotism', in R. Colls and P. Dodd (eds.), *Englishness: Politics and Culture, 1880–1920* (London, Croom Helm, 1984); J. Lawrence, 'Class and gender in the making of urban Toryism, 1880–1914', *English Historical Review*, 108 (1993), 629–52; A. Lee, 'Conservatism, traditionalism and the British working class, 1880–1918', in D. Martin and D. Rubenstein (eds.), *Ideology and the Labour Movement* (London, Croom Helm, 1979); R. Quinault, 'Lord Randolph Churchill and Tory Democracy, 1880–1885', *Historical*

Journal, 22 (1979), 141–65; E. H. H. Green, 'Radical Conservatism: the electoral genesis of tariff reform', *Historical Journal*, 28 (1985), 667–92; R. Foster, 'Tory democracy and political elitism: provincial conservatism and parliamentary Tories in the early 1880s', in A. Cosgrove and J. McGuire (eds.), *Parliament and Community* (*Historical Studies*, 14, 1983); C. Weston, 'Salisbury and the Lords, 1888–1895', *Historical Journal*, 25 (1982), 109–29.

The Conservative party in crisis, 1900–1914

Good introductions are in J. Ramsden, *The Age of Balfour*, Part 1; S. Ball, *The Conservative Party*, ch.4; M. Pugh, *The Making of Modern British Politics*, chs.5 and 7; and D. Dutton, *His Majesty's Loyal Opposition: The Unionist Party in Opposition, 1905–1915* (Liverpool, Liverpool University Press, 1992). Unlike many other periods in the history of the Conservative party, the Edwardian phase is particularly well served by historians, a feature of the acute dramas and tensions that affected the party in the years preceding the Great War.

Tariff reform was the principal source of strain and perhaps the most insightful works are A. Sykes, *Tariff Reform in British Politics, 1903–1913* (Oxford, Oxford University Press, 1979); and E. H. H. Green, *The Crisis of Conservatism*. See also A. Gollin, *Balfour's Burden: Arthur Balfour and Imperial Preference* (London, Antony Blond, 1965); R. Rempel, *Unionists Divided: Arthur Balfour, Joseph Chamberlain and the Unionist Free Traders* (London, David & Charles, 1972); N. Blewett, 'Free-Fooders, Balfourites and Whole-Hoggers: factionalism within the Unionist Party, 1906–1910', *Historical Journal*, 11 (1968), 95–124; and A. Sykes, 'The Confederacy and the purge of the Unionist Free Traders, 1906–10', *Historical Journal*, 18 (1975), 349–66. Tariff reform stimulated, and grew out of, an interest in social policy which can be studied in D. Dutton, 'The Unionist party and social policy, 1906–1914', *Historical Journal*, 24 (1981), 871–84; and J. Ridley, 'The Unionist Social Reform Committee, 1911–1914: West before the deluge', *Historical Journal*, 30 (1987), 391–413.

Struggles over the constitution, including Ireland, were another Conservative problem and may be explored in R. Jenkins, *Mr Balfour's Poodle: An Account of the Struggle between the House of Lords and the Government of Mr Asquith* (London, Collins, 1954);

N. Blewett, *The Peers, the Parties and the People: The General Elections of 1910* (London, Macmillan, 1972); G. R. Searle, *The Quest for National Efficiency* (Oxford, Oxford University Press, 1971); G. Phillips, *The Diehards: Aristocratic Society and Politics in Edwardian England* (Harvard, Harvard University Press, 1979); A. T. Q. Stewart, *The Ulster Crisis: Resistance to Home Rule, 1912–1914* (London, Faber, 1967); P. Buckland, *Irish Unionism* (Dublin, Gill & Macmillan, 1972–3); P. Bew, *Ideology and the Irish Question: Ulster Unionism and Irish Nationalism, 1912–1916* (Oxford, Oxford University Press, 1994); J. Ridley, 'The Unionist opposition and the House of Lords, 1906–10', *Parliamentary History*, 11 (1992), 238–53; R. Murphy, 'Faction in the Conservative Party and the Home Rule crisis of 1912–1914', *History*, 71 (1986), 222–34; J. Smith, 'Bluff, bluster and brinkmanship: Andrew Bonar Law and the Third Home Rule bill', *Historical Journal*, 36 (1993), 161–78; and J. Smith, ' "Paralysing the arm": Unionists and the Army Act, 1910–1914', *Parliamentary History*, 15 (1996), 191–207.

The party was also affected by the intensity of imperial and national issues. See F. Coetzee, *For Party or Country: Nationalism and the Dilemmas of Popular Conservatism in Edwardian England* (Oxford, Oxford University Press, 1990); J. A. Thompson and A. Mejia, (eds.), *Edwardian Conservatism: Five Studies in Adaptation* (London, Croom Helm, 1988); G. Phillips, 'Lord Willoughby de Broke and the politics of Radical Toryism, 1909–14', *Journal of British Studies*, 20 (1981), 205–24; A. Sykes, 'The radical right and the crisis of Conservatism before the First World War', *Historical Journal*, 26 (1983), 661–76; and B. Swartz, 'Conservatism and Caesarism, 1903–1922', in M. Langan and B. Swartz (eds.), *Crises in the British State, 1880–1930* (London, Hutchinson, 1985).

In addition, several biographies and diaries deserve mention. Of the numerous biographies of Balfour, two stand out: R. F. Mackay, *Balfour: Intellectual Statesman* (Oxford, Oxford University Press, 1985); and M. Egremont, *Balfour* (London, Collins, 1980). More dated but still valuable are R. Blake, *The Unknown Prime Minister: The Life and Times of Andrew Bonar Law, 1858–1923* (London, Eyre & Spottiswoode, 1955); and the interesting, if inappropriately titled, D. Dutton, *Austen Chamberlain: Gentleman in Politics* (Bolton, Ross Anderson, 1985). See also J. Campbell, *F. E. Smith: First Earl of Birkenhead* (London, Cape, 1983); and A. Jackson, *Sir Edward Carson* (Dublin, Irish History Studies, 1993).

Conservative hegemony established, 1914–1924

Events in this difficult and turbulent phase can be approached through J. Ramsden, *The Age of Balfour*, Part Two; S. Ball, *The Conservative Party*, chs.5 and 6; and M. Pugh, *The Making of Modern British Politics*, chs.8–12.

For the war period, one work is indispensable: J. Turner, *British Politics and the Great War: Coalition and Conflict, 1915–1918* (Yale, Yale University Press, 1992). See also C. Hazelhurst, *Politicians at War: July 1914 to May 1915* (London, Cape, 1971); K. Burk (ed.), *War and the State: The Transformation of the British Government, 1914–1919* (London, Allen & Unwin, 1982); and M. Pugh, *Electoral Reform in War and Peace, 1906–18* (London, Routledge & Kegan Paul, 1978). Among articles, see M. Pugh, 'Asquith, Bonar Law, and the First Coalition', *Historical Journal*, 17 (1974), 813–36; J. Stubbs, 'The impact of the Great War on the Conservative Party', in G. Poole and C. Cook (eds.), *The Politics of Reappraisal, 1918–39* (London, Macmillan, 1975); J. Stubbs, 'The Unionists and Ireland, 1914–1918', *Historical Journal*, 33 (1990), 867–93; R. Murphy, 'Walter Long, the Unionist Ministers, and the formation of Lloyd George's government in December 1916', *Historical Journal*, 29 (1986), 735–45; and J. Cronin, 'The British state and the structure of political opportunity', *Journal of British Studies*, 27 (1988), 199–231.

The arrival of peace and the fortunes of the Lloyd George coalition are best examined in M. Cowling, *The Impact of Labour, 1920–1924: The Beginning of Modern British Politics* (Cambridge, Cambridge University Press, 1971). See also K. O. Morgan, *Consensus and Disunity: The Lloyd George Coalition Government, 1918–1922* (Oxford, Oxford University Press, 1979); M. Kinnear, *The Fall of Lloyd George: The Political Crisis of 1922* (London, Macmillan, 1973); J. Cronin, *The Politics of State Expansion*, chs.4 and 5; G. Poole and C. Cook (eds.), *The Politics of Reappraisal, 1918–39* (London, Macmillan, 1975); J. M. McEwen, 'The Coupon Election of 1918 and Unionist members of Parliament', *Journal of Modern History*, 34 (1962), 249–73; D. H. Close, 'The collapse of resistance to democracy: Conservatives, adult suffrage and second chamber reform', *Historical Journal*, 20 (1977), 893–918; J. Turner, 'The British Commonwealth Union and the general election of 1918', *English Historical Review*, 93 (1978), 528–58; D. Rubenstein, 'Henry Page-Croft and the National Party, 1917–1922', *Journal of*

Contemporary History, 9 (1974), 129–48. For the party and Ireland, see N. Mansergh, *The Unsolved Question: The Anglo-Irish Settlement and its Undoing, 1912–1972* (Yale, Yale University Press, 1991); D. G. Boyce, *Englishmen and Irish Troubles, 1918–1922* (London, Cape, 1972); and C. Townsend, *The British Campaign in Ireland, 1919–1921* (Oxford, Oxford University Press, 1975).

The importance of Baldwin is barely touched on here, but the best insights are in J. Ramsden, *The Age of Balfour*, Part Three; S. Ball, *The Conservative Party*, ch. 6; also Ball's *Baldwin and the Conservative Party: The Crisis of 1929–1931* (Yale, Yale University Press, 1988), ch.1; and his 'The Conservative dominance 1918–1940', *Modern History Review*, 3 (1991), 109–29; R. Jenkins, *Baldwin* (London, Collins, 1987); R. Colls and P. Dodd (eds.), *Englishness: Politics and Culture, 1880–1920* (London, Croom Helm, 1986); C. Cook, *The Age of Alignment: Electoral Politics in Britain, 1922–29* (London, Macmillan, 1975); B. Coleman, 'The Conservative party and the frustration of the extreme right', in A. Thorpe (ed.), *The Failure of Political Extremism in Inter-War Britain* (Exeter, Exeter University Press, 1989). Three particularly important pieces are R. McKibben, 'Class and conventional wisdom: the Conservative party and the public of inter-war Britain', in *The Ideologies of Class: Social Relations in Britain, 1880–1950* (Oxford, Oxford University Press, 1991); R. Self, 'Conservative reunion and the general election of 1923: a reassessment', *Twentieth Century British History*, 3 (1992), 249–73; and P. Williamson, 'The doctrinal politics of Stanley Baldwin', in M. Bentley (ed.), *Public and Private Doctrine* (Cambridge, Cambridge University Press, 1993).

Index